P9-EEH-195

BOATING®

MAGAZINE'S

One Minute Guide to the Nautical Rules of the Road

CHARLIE WING

International Marine/
Ragged Mountain Press
A Division of The **McGraw-Hill** *Companies*

Copyright © 1998 International Marine

10 9 8 7 6 5 4

All rights reserved. The publisher takes no responsibility for the use of any of the materials or methods described in this book, nor for the products thereof. The name "International Marine" and the International Marine logo are trademarks of The McGraw-Hill Companies. Printed in the United States of America.

Boating® is a registered trademark of Hachette Filipacchi Magazines, Inc. used under license by International Marine/Ragged Mountain Press.

Library of Congress Cataloging-in-Publication Data
Wing, Charles, 1939–
Boating® magazine's one minute guide to the nautical rules of the road/Charlie Wing.
p. cm.
Includes index.
ISBN 0-07-071094-5 (pbk.)
1. Inland navigation—Law and legislation—United States—Popular works. 2. Rules of the road at sea—Popular Works.
I. Boating (Chicago, Ill.) II. Title
KF2566.Z9W53 1998
343.7309'66—dc21 98-17629
CIP

Questions regarding the content of this book should be addressed to:
International Marine
P.O. Box 220
Camden, ME 04843

Questions regarding the ordering of this book should be addressed to:
The McGraw-Hill Companies
Customer Service Department
P.O. Box 547
Blacklick, OH 43004
Retail customers: 1-800-262-4729
Bookstores: 1-800-233-4726

Visit us on the World Wide Web at www.internationalmarine.com

Printed by R. R. Donnelley, Crawfordsville, IN
Design and page layout by Julianna Nielsen, Sloane Publications
Illustrations by Charlie Wing

Here lies the body of Michael O'Day
Who died maintaining his Right of Way.
He was right, dead right, as he sailed along,
But he's just as dead as if he'd been wrong

Contents

Section 2 *International and Inland Rules* **43**

Introduction

The *International Regulations for the Prevention of Collision at Sea* (COLREGS) are the "Rules of the Road" on the water. These Rules, and the essentially identical *United States Inland Rules,* apply to all boats, regardless of type or size, on all seas and on most U.S. bays, inlets, rivers, and waterways connected to the sea.

In spite of the serious consequences of boating accidents, less than ten percent of boaters have an even rudimentary familiarity with the Rules. The International Maritime Organization estimates that over eighty percent of all boating accidents are due to human error and that most stem from the failure to comply with one or more provisions of the Rules.

The fact that most small boat operators lack a working knowledge of the Rules is understandable. Like most legal documents, the Rules appear to be quite complex. In translation, however, the Rules can be readily understood by anyone who knows port from starboard. We offer this little book as a painless introduction.

By law, all vessels of twelve meters or more in length that operate in U.S. Inland Waters are required to carry an up-to-date copy of the Rules. Courts have also ruled smaller boats negligent for not carrying them. While this book explains the Rules, you should still carry a copy of the official publication, *Navigation Rules, International–Inland,* on board. You can find this publication for a nominal price at chandleries and for free over the Internet at: *www.uscg.mil/hq/gm/nmc/navrules.pdf.*

The author would like to thank numerous Coast Guard personnel for their input, Mr. Wesley Moore for his insightful review, Jon Eaton for his patience, Julianna Nielsen for her wonderful design, and finally, *Boating Magazine* for bringing this book to the boating community.

How to Use this Book

Inside the front cover you will find the One-Minute Guide, a "decision tree" indicating the action to be taken in any boating situation. Section One (pages 9–42) of the text presents the general principles of the Rules, and, beginning on page 18, follows the outline of the decision tree, helping you identify your situation. Throughout Section One, you will find marginal references to the appropriate Rule numbers. Section Two (pages 43–103) presents the full text of the Rules and offers further insight into their finer points.

The best way to learn the Rules is to begin following them. Read Section One thoroughly, then apply its principles to boating situations as they occur. You will soon find that the Rules make perfect (i.e., common) sense. Affix the One-Minute Guide Decision Tree to your cockpit as a ready reference, and you should never be confounded again.

Italicized text that appears in discussions of the rules beginning on page 43 indicates where the Inland Rules differ substantially from international rules (COLREGS).

SECTION 1

What Every Boater Needs to Know

UNDERLYING PRINCIPLES

Purpose of the Rules

The purpose of the Rules is not, as is commonly thought, to grant one boat the right-of-way over another. The idea of a "right-of-way" fell out of favor as it became clear, through court cases, that avoiding a collision between two boats requires the participation of both parties. The purpose of the Rules is to present, in a situation where danger of collision between two boats exists, guidelines for the actions required of both. Under the Rules, one boat is designated the *stand-on vessel;* the other the *give-way vessel* (see page 10). These designations carry obligations for each vessel to act in a specified way to avoid collision.

It is important to note that the Rules never address situations involving more than two boats. Whenever the possibility of collision exists between more than two boats, common sense must be your principal guide.

Important Definitions

3

Vessel: anything that carries people or cargo on or in the water, including kayaks, personal watercraft, sea planes, and super tankers.

Power-driven vessel: any vessel underway with an engine that does not fall into any of the other special categories defined below.

Sailing vessel: a sailboat underway with sails (not using an engine).

Vessel engaged in fishing: any boat fishing with equipment which limits its ability to maneuver (nets, trawls, etc.).

Vessel not under command: a vessel unable to maneuver as required by the Rules, due to mechanical breakdown or any other reason.

Vessel restricted in her ability to maneuver: a vessel that, due to the nature of her work, cannot maneuver easily. Examples include buoy tenders, dredges, dive boats, minesweepers, and tugs with difficult tows.

Vessel constrained by her draft: a vessel that may go aground if it deviates from its course. (Note that the Inland Rules do not contain this definition.)

Underway: not anchored, grounded, or otherwise attached to shore. A boat does not have to be moving either through the water or over the ground to be *underway*.

Restricted visibility: any condition that reduces visibility, including fog, heavy rain, snow, and smoke.

Give-way vessel: the vessel obligated to keep out of the way of the other.

Stand-on vessel: the vessel obligated to maintain its course and speed.

Sailboat or Sailing Vessel?

When is a sailboat considered a "sailing vessel"? Cruising sailors often "motorsail"—that is, they run their engines to augment the wind. Rule 25(e) requires motorsailing sailboats (except those of less than twelve meters, under Inland Rules) to display a cone, apex down. Unfortunately, they rarely do so. You can usually tell that a boat is motorsailing by observing its exhaust.

Making the distinction between "sailing" and "motorsailing" is important because, under the Rules, running the engine turns a sailboat into a power-driven vessel. Be careful when crossing paths with a motorsailer, however. Many sailors think a sailboat is a "sailing vessel" as long as it has a mast and sails!

Fishing Boat or Fishing Vessel?

When is a fishing boat not considered a "fishing vessel"? The Rules make it clear that when not engaged in the act of fishing, fishing boats have the same status as any power-driven vessel. But what about sport fishermen, lobstermen, and crabbers?

The distinction lies in the degree to which fishing gear hampers the maneuverability of a vessel. Trolling a light line does not hamper it; however, trawling or dragging a heavy net does. Although a lobsterman running to his next buoy is not hampered, when pulling up a string of traps with his hauler, he is effectively moored to the bottom.

Common courtesy dictates that you give these hardworking men and women a wide berth, so that they can concentrate on catching your dinner.

Do the Rules Apply to Me?

In a word—yes. The *International Regulations for the Prevention of Collision at Sea* (COLREGS) apply to all vessels, from kayaks to ocean-liners, on all of the oceans and bodies of water outside the magenta (red) Demarcation Line printed on charts. The *United States Inland Rules* apply on the Great Lakes, Western Rivers, waterways, and specific bays inside the Demarcation Line.

COLREGS or Racing Rules?

What happens when two sailboats collide while racing? A 1995 court case *(Juno SRL v. S/V Endeavour*) established that the International Yacht Racing Rules (IYRR), or whatever set of racing rules the sailboats are racing under, take precedence over the COLREGS during a race.

The two sailboats, *Charles Jourdan* and *Endeavour,* were racing in the Bay of St. Tropez. Approaching a mark, the *Jourdan* assumed it had the "right-of-way" under IYRR Rule 37.1, "a windward yacht shall keep clear of a leeward yacht." The *Endeavour* at first refused to keep clear. When she belatedly altered course to windward, her boom struck the *Jourdan*, causing $10,000 damage. The race committee, applying the IYRR rule, found the *Endeavour* at fault.

The *Jourdan* subsequently filed suit for damages in district court. The district court threw out the IYRR ruling, finding that the *Jourdan* had been an overtaking vessel under COLREGS Rule 13 and thus required to keep clear.

On appeal, however, the first circuit court overturned the district court's ruling, saying: "Nothing in their history, or in the public policy issues that led to their enactment, indicates that they (the COLREGS) were meant to regulate voluntary private sports activity in which the participants have waived their application and in which no interference with nonparticipating maritime traffic is implicated."

The case applies only to yachts participating in a race. It does not apply to other vessels in the vicinity that are not participating in the race. Thus, in a conflict between racing and nonracing boats, the COLREGS still rule.

How Am I Responsible?

RULE

2

Everyone having to do with the operation of your boat—its owner, master (person in charge underway), and crew—is responsible for obeying the Rules, as well as for using caution, good sense, and good seamanship. However, the Rules acknowledge that they cannot cover every conceivable situation. If absolutely necessary to avoid immediate danger, you are, in fact, required to break the Rules. In other words, use your head for the purpose intended, not as a hat rack.

Does My Boat Need a Lookout?

RULE

5

Absolutely! Your boat is required to maintain a lookout for the possibility of collision at all times and to use all available methods and equipment (eyes, ears, radio, and radar, if installed). Of course, if you are the only person on board, then you have to serve as master, crew, and lookout all at the same time. If there is more than one person aboard, however, the master should appoint a separate lookout.

Do Single-Handed Sailors Have the Right to Zzzzz?

In a 1984 court case (*Granholm v. TFL Express)*, the court found a single-handed racer negligent for taking a thirty-minute nap.

The yacht, *Granholm*, was participating in a qualifying sail for a transatlantic race. With the boat on autopilot, and with all required navigation lights showing, the owner scanned the horizon for ships, set a thirty-minute timer, and went below for a nap. Meanwhile, the *TFL Express* was on autopilot, making eighteen knots; the mate was plotting her position, and the "lookout" was making tea. The *Express* came up from behind and ran the *Granholm* down.

The owner of the *Granholm* sued the *Express* for her failure to maintain a proper lookout (Rule 5), and for neglecting, as the overtaking vessel, her obligation to keep clear (Rule 13). The court agreed, but placed equal blame on the single-hander, saying, "The obligation to maintain a proper lookout falls upon great vessels and small alike."

In other words, if single-handed sailing prevents one from maintaining a "proper lookout," as defined by the Rules, then the very act is negligent. Single-handers beware.

What Is a Safe Speed?

You must never exceed a safe speed for the conditions. The Rules do not define "safe speed," but the courts have often interpreted it as the speed that would allow a boat to avoid collision. Factors you must consider include: visibility conditions, background lights, traffic intensity, maneuverability of your vessel, maneuverability of other vessels, wind and current, navigational hazards, depth of water, and the limitations of radar.

A Titanic Error in Judgment

Everyone knows the substance of the *Titanic* disaster, but do you know which single COLREGS rule she broke?

Captain E. J. Smith, with over 2,000,000 miles under his keel, was given the honor of commanding the *Titanic* on her maiden voyage. Amidst great hoopla and newspaper stories citing the *Titanic* as proof of man's mastery over nature, she embarked from Southampton, England, on April 10, 1912, bound for New York. Her owners were anxious for her to show a good turn of speed on this, her very first outing. Captain Smith had another reason—this was to be his last trip before retiring.

There is little doubt that the pressure for a speedy Atlantic crossing clouded the judgment of the able Captain. On consecutive days, the *Titanic* ripped off 386 miles, 519 miles, then 546 miles. On the 14th, at 22½ knots, she was approaching her theoretical top speed of twenty-four knots.

Iceberg warnings began to come in from other vessels. At least eleven warnings were received, but iceberg warnings were common at this time of year. That Captain Smith received the warnings there is no doubt. Being a prudent mariner, he altered course slightly to the southwest.

At 11:40 P.M., the lookout in the crow's nest sounded the alarm, "Iceberg dead ahead!" The helm was put hard-a-starboard immediately. The *Titanic* responded—but not quickly enough. Less than forty seconds after the alarm, the iceberg struck the *Titanic* a glancing blow, punching a 300-foot series of holes beneath her waterline.

Have you guessed which COLREGS rule Captain Smith broke?

"Every vessel shall at all times proceed at a safe speed . . ." *(Rule 6)*

WHEN YOU MEET ANOTHER BOAT

Determining Risk of Collision

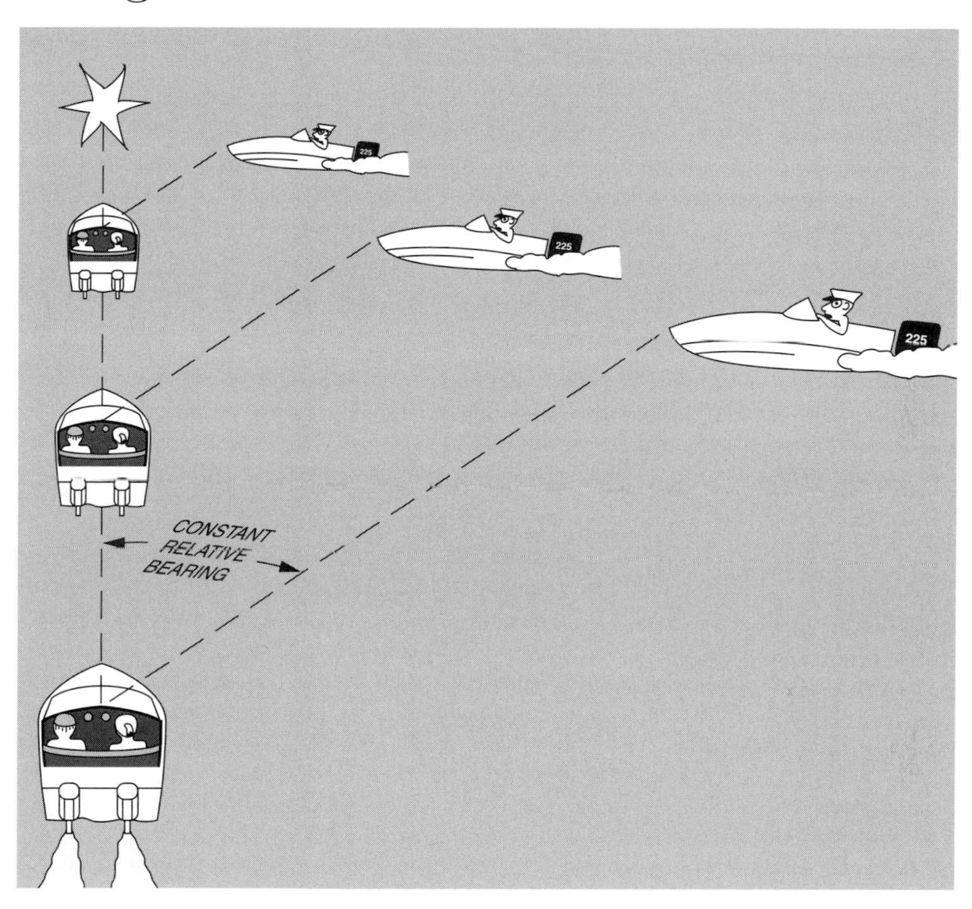

Collision with another boat is possible when the compass bearing to it remains constant as your two boats converge. The rule specifically says that you must use all available means, including radar if you have it, to aid in this determination. Fortunately, for small boat operators without radar, a relative bearing sighted against a stanchion or other fixed part of your boat may substitute for a compass bearing, as long as you maintain constant course and speed. If there is any doubt at all, consider that collision is possible.

You Assumed What?

The collision of the *Stockholm* and the *Andrea Doria,* on the night of July 25, 1956, serves as a study in poor judgment. The Swedish-American *Stockholm* was on a course from New York City to the Nantucket Lightship, in conditions of good visibility. At the same time, the Italian *Andrea Doria,* operating in a dense fog, had passed the Lightship and was headed for New York. Captain Calamax of the *Andrea Doria* took his usual fog precautions: He positioned a lookout at the bow, closed all watertight hatches, and placed the engine room on alert. He reduced speed, but only from twenty-three to 21.8 knots, because he was running late and knew that any significant target would appear on his radar.

At 10:40 P.M., a target appeared. Captain Calamai, assuming the blip to be just a fishing boat, neglected to plot its course and speed, and further, ignored the time-honored custom of passing port-to-port. Had he known that the other vessel was coming nearly straight at him at nineteen knots, he probably would have taken early and substantial action by turning at least twenty degrees to starboard.

At 10:48 P.M., the third officer of the *Stockholm* saw on his radar a vessel (the *Andrea Doria)* twelve miles ahead. At ten miles, he plotted the twelve- and ten-mile relative positions and figured that the other vessel would pass one-half mile to one mile to his port. Since there was no fog where he was, he also assumed that he would soon see the other vessel's navigation lights. When, at four miles, there were still no lights, he assumed that either the other vessel's lights were broken, or that the vessel was a warship on maneuvers.

One minute later, the *Stockholm* entered the thick fog. Three minutes later, the *Stockholm*'s lookout sighted the *Andrea Doria*'s lights ahead to port, and the third officer turned his ship twenty degrees to starboard. At nearly the same instant, Captain Calamai spotted the *Stockholm*, and ordered the *Andrea Doria* to turn to port. The *Stockholm* struck the *Andrea Doria* on her starboard side, sending her to the bottom.

Captain Calamai's turn to port might be questioned, but the more important lesson to be learned from this accident is to never assume that you know what another vessel is doing.

Action to Avoid Collision

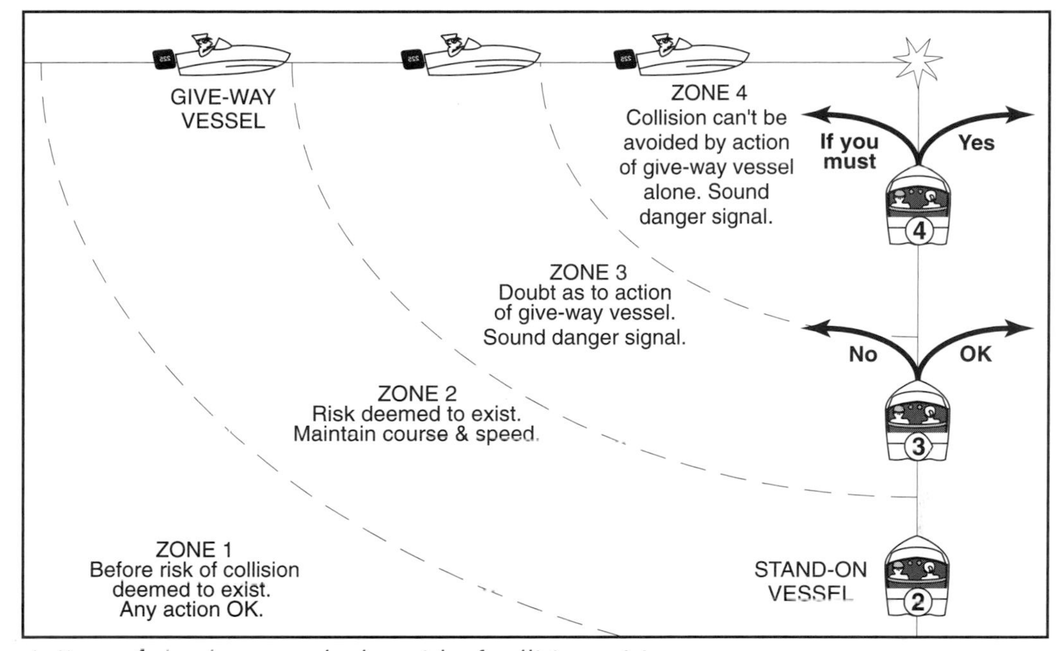

Actions of stand-on vessel when risk of collision exists

The give-way boat's action to avoid collision must be early and large enough to assure the stand-on boat that she is taking action. Given room to maneuver, changing course is better than changing speed because it is more immediately obvious to the other boat. A course change large enough to be obvious would present a different view of the give-way boat in daylight and different navigation lights at night. A large enough speed change would be throttling down to no-wake speed or even stopping.

The stand-on vessel is obligated to maintain course and speed. In a collision situation, the actions permitted or required of the stand-on vessel take place in four stages.

1. Before the risk of collision exists, either boat may maneuver as it pleases.
2. Once risk of collision exists, the stand-on boat must maintain its course and speed.
3. If it seems to the stand-on boat that the other boat is not going to keep out of the way, then she should sound the danger signal (five short blasts) and *may* take any action *except* a turn to port for a give-way boat on her port.
4. If the situation develops to the point where a collision can no longer be avoided by the action of the give-way boat alone, the stand-on boat is *required* to sound the danger signal and take the most effective action it can to avoid the collision.

ONE-MINUTE GUIDE DECISION TREE

The decision tree found on the inside front cover acts as a quick reference when approaching another vessel. If you can see the other boat, use the "In-Sight Situation" guidelines. Begin at the top and move down the left-hand column until you find the circumstance that pertains to you. If you are in an area of restricted visibility, use the bottom portion of the tree. The following information will help you identify your situation.

Traffic Separation Schemes

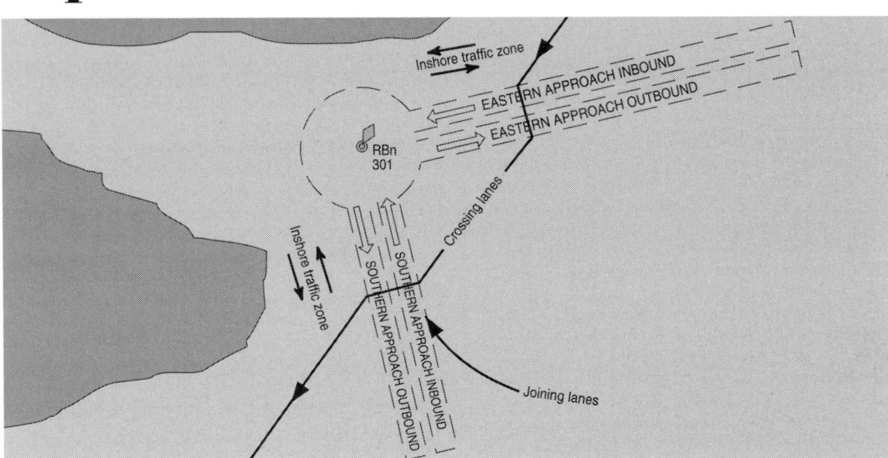

Traffic separation schemes (TSS) are inbound and outbound traffic lanes, divided by separation lines or zones, and printed in magenta on charts. Their purpose is to provide one-way lanes for large ships into and out of major ports. Between the traffic lanes and any adjacent land masses, you will usually find inshore traffic zones (labeled as such on your chart). Sailboats, fishing boats, and all boats under twenty meters (65'7") are free to use these inshore traffic zones, and in any case, are to stay clear of any ship using a traffic lane. If you must cross a traffic lane, do so quickly, far away from other vessels, and at a right angle to the flow of traffic.

Note that vessel traffic services, found only in the Inland Rules, are roughly equivalent to traffic separation schemes.

In a Narrow Channel or Fairway

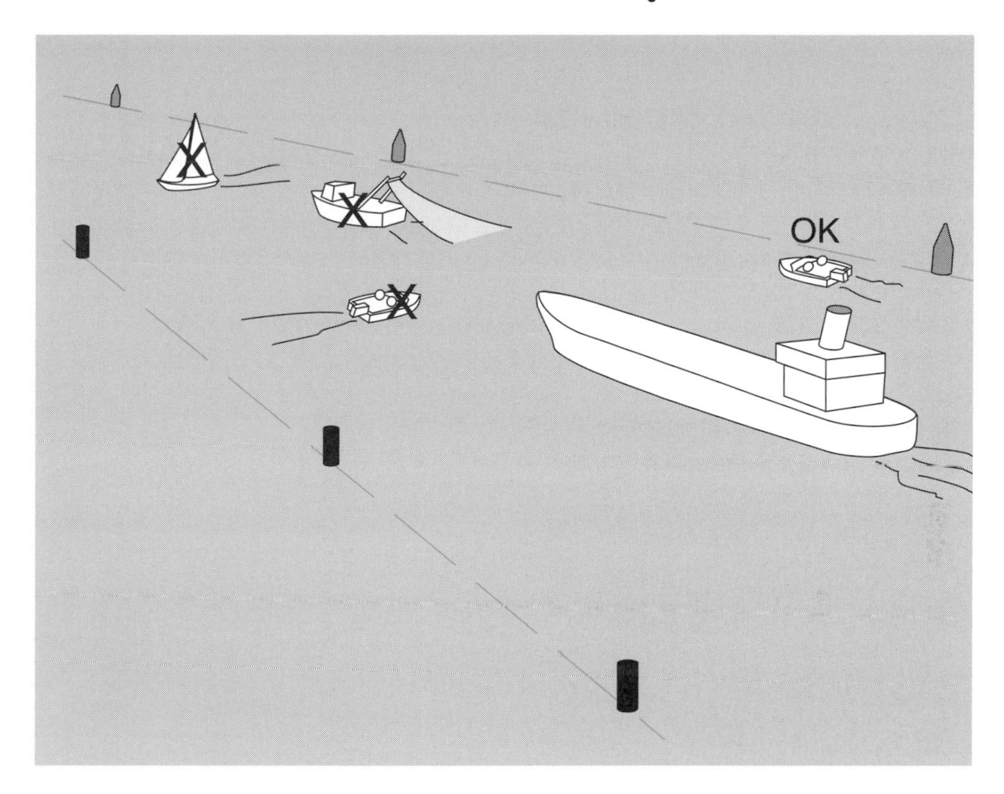

A channel is a safe route between hazards, or a deeper route through shallow water. It is "narrow" when boats in it are severely limited in room to maneuver. A fairway is the thoroughfare between docks and piers in a harbor. In general, stay out of narrow channels and fairways that are trafficked heavily by large ships and tugs. When in a narrow channel or fairway, however:

- Stay as close as possible to the starboard side.
- Sailboats, fishing boats, and boats of less than twenty meters should stay clear of boats that are confined to the channel.
- Do not cross the channel if it will interfere with a boat confined to the channel.
- Do not anchor in the channel.
- Sound a prolonged (four to six second) blast when approaching a bend or other obscured area. Boats approaching in the opposite direction should answer with the same signal.

Kayaks and Other Speed Bumps

With the exception of the lighting requirements for Vessels Under Oars (Rule 25), there is no mention in either the COLREGS or the Inland Rules of rowboats, kayaks, canoes, or other human-powered vessels. The reason for this apparent oversight is that the Rules were developed for the purpose of preventing collision between ships on the high seas. It is only recently that one has seen kayaks on open waters. With the increasing appearance of what powerboaters are fond of calling "speed bumps," it is appropriate to consider how the Rules—or lack thereof—apply to these little craft.

First, which of the rules, if any, *do* apply to human-powered craft? Rules 1 through 11 and Rule 13 apply to all vessels, regardless of size or means of propulsion. Therefore, human-powered vessels must observe the general rules of *responsibility, maintaining a lookout, not exceeding a safe speed, determining risk of collision, and taking proper action to avoid collision.* Of particular importance, however, are Rules 9 and 10.

Rule 9 Narrow Channels
9 (b) "A vessel of less than twenty meters in length ... shall not impede the passage of a vessel which can safely navigate only within a narrow channel or fairway."

Rule 10 Traffic Separation Schemes
10(d) " A vessel ... of less than twenty meters in length ... may use inshore traffic zones."
10(j) "A vessel of less than twenty meters in length ... shall not impede the safe passage of a power-driven vessel following a traffic lane."

In other words, human-powered vessels should, whenever possible, stay out of channels used by large vessels.

Second, what about situations where the Rules are not specific? In discussions with U.S. Coast Guard personnel, two principles are repeatedly cited:

Maneuverability
Most of the Rules are based on the unstated principle of relative maneuverability; that is, the vessel having the greater ability to avoid collision under the circumstances is generally charged with keeping clear. Unfortunately, one cannot generalize and say that human-powered vessels are either more or less maneuverable than other craft. Kayaks and rowboats may be able to spin on a dime, but they are also slow. The relative maneuverabilities of a kayak and a larger vessel can thus depend on size, speed, wind, waves, current, depth of water, and navigation hazards, to name just a few.

(continued)

Negligent Operation

The civil law concept of "negligent operation" can always be applied. Operating a vessel (or a motor vehicle, for that matter) without consideration for conditions, without reasonable precaution, and in violation of common sense, all constitute negligent operation.

When you combine these two principles, it is usually clear which of two vessels should stay clear in any given situation. A few examples should illustrate the point:

1. *High speed runabout on a collision course with a kayak.* Due to its much greater speed, the runabout could easily run down the kayak, regardless of evasive action by the kayak. The runabout should probably stay clear, as it must in an overtaking situation.

2. *Rowing dinghy crossing a harbor in a wind.* A rowing dinghy provides a common means of transportation between a moored or anchored vessel and shore. In a wind, progress can be slow enough that its operator cannot reasonably be expected to anticipate all of the vessel traffic he will meet on the way. Larger vessels should take this into account when applying the Rules. On the other hand, a freighter or tanker is large enough to be seen far in advance, in which case the dinghy operator should delay his crossing.

3. *Kayaker riding the bow wave of a larger vessel.* While great sport for the kayaker, it is also a distraction to the skipper of the larger vessel, who must consider the proximity of the kayak in maneuvering. Surfing another vessel's bow wave—at least in close proximity—is a clear case of negligent operation.

Look Out for Floating Objects

The following story illustrates the dangers of a small vessel sharing a narrow channel with larger vessels: On the evening of December 19, 1993, a pilot was lining up the bulk carrier *Sealnes* to pass under the Lions Gate Bridge on its way into Vancouver Harbor. At the same time, *Mr. Fission,* a thirty-foot dive tender, was headed out of the harbor. *Mr. Fission* was having engine trouble, so instead of crossing to the starboard side of the channel, as required, he decided to hug the port shore while he worked on his engine. The current in the channel was making 2.8 knots, but since it was running in a favorable direction, the captain decided not to anchor while the crew worked on the engine. Distracted by the engine repairs, the captain failed to notice that the strong current was drawing him out into the main channel.

The vessel traffic service (VTS) in Vancouver, which monitors and directs traffic in the controlled traffic lanes, advised the *Sealnes* of two radar targets in the channel ahead. The pilot assumed these to be the two tugs he expected to greet him. In fact, the tugs in question were so close to each other that they appeared on radar to be a single target; the second radar target was actually *Mr. Fission.*

The chief officer of the *Sealnes*, standing on deck, heard a noise over the starboard bow. When he looked, he saw *Mr. Fission,* upended, with her three crew in the water. The *Sealnes* had run down *Mr. Fission* without either vessel seeing the other.

What went wrong? The captain of *Mr. Fission* should have alerted the VTS and area traffic of his predicament, his location, and the fact that he was on the wrong side of the channel. He also should have maintained a proper lookout while repairing his engine. The pilot and crew of the *Sealnes* falsely assumed that the two targets reported by the VTS were the two tugs they were expecting. Rather than rely entirely on the VTS, they should have had their own lookout.

Overtaking

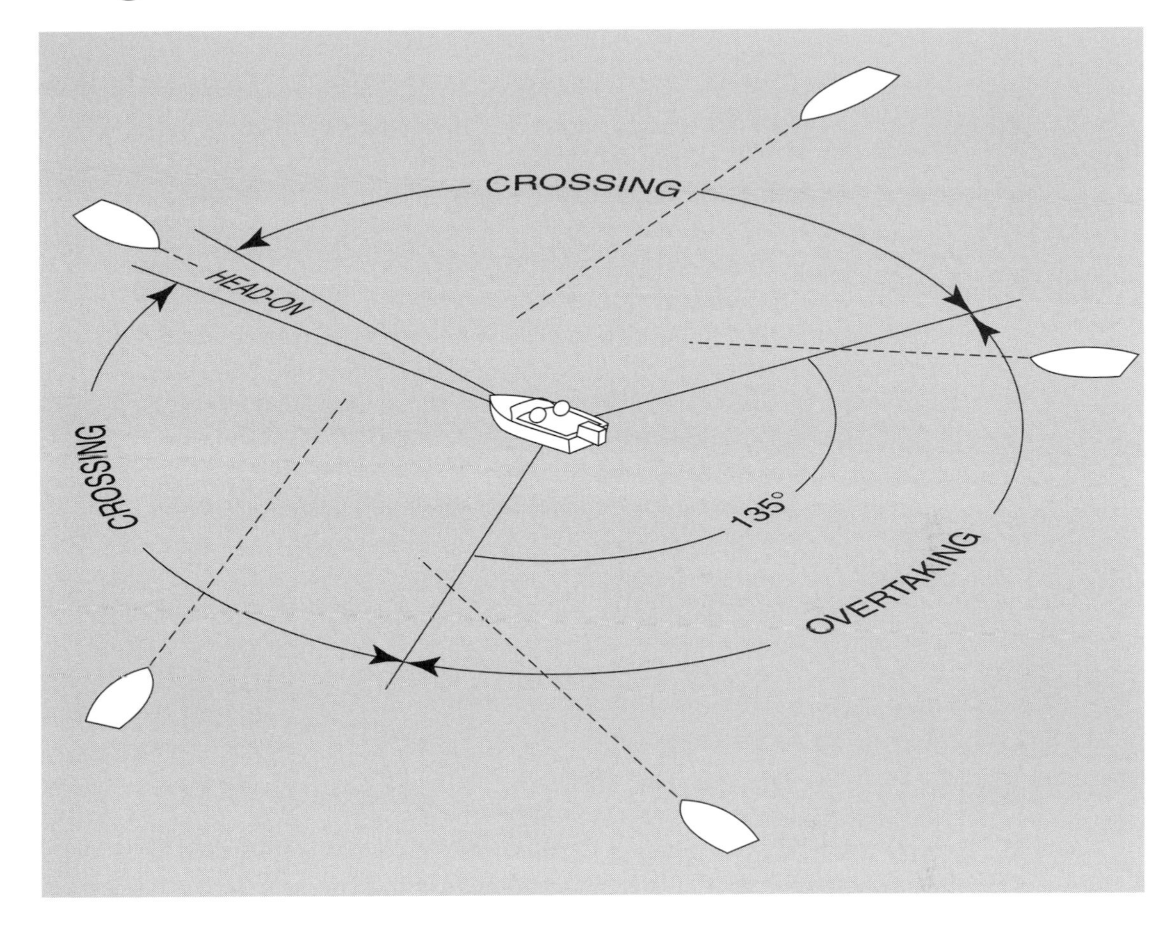

You are overtaking another boat when you approach it within the 135° arc of its sternlight. If there is any doubt as to whether you are overtaking, assume that you are.

When an overtaken boat must take action to be safely passed (as in a narrow channel), both boats must first reach agreement through sound signals (see pages 30–31) or via VHF radio (Inland only). The burden is on the overtaking boat to steer clear until it is totally past and safely clear of the overtaken boat.

Haste Makes Waste

A pleasure yacht and a large ferry were proceeding in the same direction down a narrow channel. To allow room for a third vessel, which was approaching from the opposite direction, the ferry passed the yacht close on the yacht's port side. The hydrodynamic effects caused by her large displacement and the suction of her propellers pulled the yacht into the side of the ferry, inflicting damage. Who was at fault?

- The ferry was an overtaking vessel and thus required to keep clear (Rule 13).
- The ferry should have reduced her speed in order to delay her passing (Rule 8).
- Since safe passage required action by the overtaken yacht, the ferry should have indicated her intention to pass and waited for the yacht to signal agreement (Rule 9).

"Is this not one of those cases of three or more vessels, and thus not subject to the Rules?" you might ask. Remember that, when the Rules cannot be applied in a confusing situation involving more than two vessels, you are to apply common sense. Here, common sense would dictate delaying the overtaking until the approaching vessel had safely passed, thus avoiding the three-vessel situation.

Power-Driven Vessels Meeting Head-On

14

Power-driven vessels meeting head-on should each alter course to starboard and pass port-to-port. Head-on is when you see: 1) in daylight, another boat headed nearly straight at you, or 2) at night, both sidelights or the masthead lights of the other nearly in line. If you have the slightest doubt whether the situation is head-on, assume that it is.

Exception: Power-driven vessels proceeding downbound on the Great Lakes and Western Rivers have the right-of-way over upbound boats and should propose the manner of passage via sound signals or VHF radio. Also, both upbound and downbound power-driven vessels have the right-of-way over all types of crossing vessels.

Who's on First?

On April 12, 1991, the 584-foot *Sersou* was downbound on the St. Lawrence River, moving at eight knots. At the same time, the 714-foot *Silver Isle* was upbound at 12.5 knots.

At 1803, the two vessels were about 8⁄10 of a mile apart, and approaching a slight bend in the channel. Suddenly, the *Sersou* developed a swing to port. Whether the swing was due to helmsman error or to hydrodynamic effect is not known, but it was obvious enough to strike terror into the heart of the pilot of the *Silver Isle,* who had been expecting a normal port-to-port passing. The recorded conversation between the two French-speaking pilots reminds one of the Abbott and Costello "Who's on First?" routine:

(English Translation)
1803:40 *(Sersou)* "Watch me closely, I'm hard-a-starboard."
1803:53 *(Silver Isle)* "Are you OK to pass? Two whistles [under the Inland Rules, the signal for a starboard-to-starboard passing]."
1803:59 *(Sersou)* "No, not two whistles, she's coming back."
1804:03 *(Silver Isle)* "It's too late ... two whistles."
1804:07 *(Sersou)* "OK, two whistles"
1804:20 *(Sersou)* "Two whistles, eh?"
1804:21 *(Silver Isle)* "What did you say?"
1804:23 *(Sersou)* "What are you doing there, two whistles?"
1804:25 *(Silver Isle)* "Two whistles."
1804:28 *(Silver Isle)* "I'm going hard-a-port, hard-a-port."
1804:32 *(Sersou)* "I'm hard-a-port too."
[CRUNCH]
1804:54 *(Sersou)* "You told me ... you asked me to go to port."

What the recorded conversation doesn't show is that the *Silver Isle's* Officer of the Watch (OOW), not understanding French, became alarmed at the developing situation and ran to get the master. Since the OOW couldn't explain to the master what was happening, and, since the pilot was on the radio with the other pilot, the master unwittingly countered the pilot's instructions, ordering the *Silver Isle's* helm to starboard.

The lesson here is, clearly, the importance of communication in avoiding collision.

Power-Driven Vessels Crossing

A boat crossing your path from your starboard side should stand on (maintain course and speed), while a boat approaching you on your port side must give way. The give-way boat should not cross ahead of the stand-on boat. Remember, a stand-on boat on your starboard side sees your green "go" light, while a boat on your port side sees your red "stop" light. Conversely, you see the "go" light of a boat on your port, and the "stop" light of a vessel on your starboard. *Exception: On the Great Lakes and Western Rivers, any type of vessel crossing a river must keep out of the way of a power boat ascending or descending the river, regardless of port and starboard.*

Two Sailboats Meeting

First, a sailboat is a "sailing vessel" only when she is using her sails as her only source of propulsion. Next, the "tack" of a sailboat is the side opposite that on which the mainsail is carried (or, on a square-rigged vessel, the largest fore-and-aft sail). Given these definitions, the rule governing sailboats is simple:

- When two sailboats are on different tacks, the boat on the port tack must keep clear.
- When two sailboats are on the same tack, the boat to windward (upwind) must keep clear.
- If a sailboat on a port tack is uncertain of the tack of an upwind sailboat, she must still keep clear.

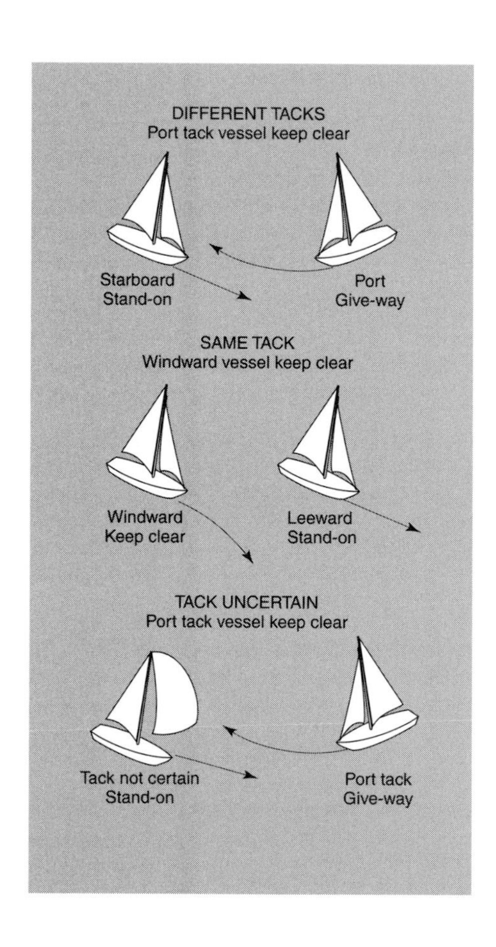

Mixed Vessel Types—The Pecking Order

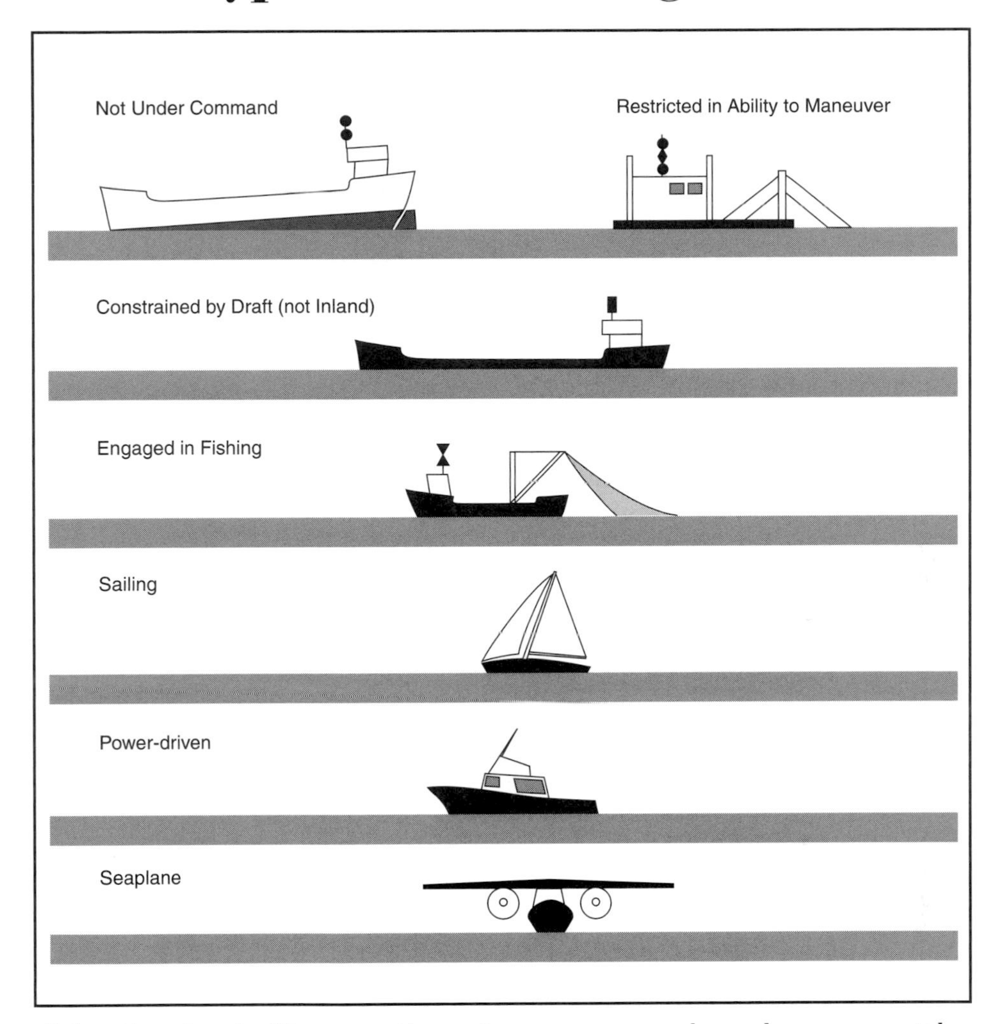

Other than in a traffic separation scheme, a narrow channel, or an overtaking situation, you must observe a "pecking order." Find your boat in the illustration. You must stay clear of all vessel types above you; all vessel types below you must keep clear of you. Vessels not under command and vessels restricted in ability to maneuver share the top billing.

In order to claim privileged status, a vessel must display its appropriate shapes by day and lights by night. Failure to display such signals may get the privileged vessel in trouble; however, it will not let you off the hook if you tangle with them.

Fog Situation

All of the rules above assume that you see the other boat. In or near an area of restricted visibility, you must slow to a safe speed for the visibility, and sound fog signals. If you detect another boat by radar or by sound, you must evaluate the risk of collision. If risk does exist (decreasing range at constant bearing), you must take avoiding action, BUT DO NOT:

- turn to port for a boat forward (unless you are overtaking it);
- turn toward a boat abeam or aft your beam.

Unless you are absolutely certain that there is no risk of collision when you hear the fog signal of a boat forward, you must reduce your speed to bare steerageway or, if necessary, stop. Important: When (and if) your vessels become visible to each other, you both go back to the in-sight rules.

A Message from the Bridge

Captain William Gribbin is a pilot for the harbor of Portland, Maine, one of the busiest oil ports on the U. S. East Coast. His job is to bring 800-foot tankers through the inner harbor to their berths. The message he sends to recreational boaters could come from the pilot or captain of any large vessel.

" I start popping Rolaids at Portland Head Light. That's when the acid really starts churning. Small boaters have no idea what it's like to maneuver an 800-foot tanker. They think, with all our power and radar and what not, that we have complete control—that we can turn to avoid them or even stop. Inside Portland Head Light, we are restricted to a speed of four knots. We have 12,000 horses, but at four knots, a loaded tanker takes a quarter of a mile and seven minutes to stop! Moreover, once we put the engines in reverse, we lose all steerage. To make an analogy, it's like pushing a thirty-foot Sea Ray with a one-horse trolling motor and steering with a shingle.

(continued)

We also have a blind zone up front. We can't see anything directly in front of us for about 600 feet. If a little guy disappears in front of us, I can only pop another Rolaid and pray that I won't see wreckage in our wake. Even if I could see that we were about to run him down, should I put the helm hard over and run the risk of dumping 100,000 barrels of crude oil into the environment? Sometimes, those are the only two choices I have.

My favorite rule is the narrow channel rule, Rule 9. It says that sailboats, fishing boats, and boats of less than twenty meters shall not impede the passage of a vessel that can safely navigate only within a narrow channel. What does 'shall not impede' mean? To me it means:

- Don't anchor in the channel.
- Don't troll or drift in the channel.
- Don't cross in front of me.
- Don't pass between me and my tugs.
- In fact, don't come within 250 feet of me!

Now, about radar. Even on open waters, boaters should never assume that we see them. Sure, we have fancy radars—several, in fact. But you have to reflect the radar signal back in order for us to see you. Even with a good radar reflector, most small boats don't show up beyond a mile or two. Without a reflector, we're lucky to pick them up at a quarter mile. When waves kick up, we have to turn up the sea-clutter control to eliminate reflections from the nearest waves. We are essentially eliminating all reflections from close range. So much for kayakers! I have never seen a kayak on radar.

I'm also amazed at how boaters use their radios. They have VHF, they have CB, they even have cell-phones. They call each other to see how the fishing is; they call to see if Joe remembered to bring the beer; but they never call us. All large vessels are required by the regulations to listen to VHF CH13 and CH16. If you want to tell us what you are doing or ask us what we are doing, please, please call us on CH13 or CH16!"

COMMUNICATIONS BETWEEN BOATS

Sounds—Blow Your Own Horn

The Rules state that when a maneuvering action is required to avoid collision, the vessels involved must use sound signals to communicate their intentions. Since adoption of the Vessel Bridge-to-Bridge Radiotelephone Act, the more common practice under Inland Rules is to reach understanding on VHF radio CH13. The roots of the practice can still be heard, however, when captains propose passing on "one whistle" (port side–to–port side) or "two whistles" (starboard side–to–starboard side). The table below shows the sound signals required under both International and Inland Rules.

Maneuvering and Warning Signals in Sight (• = one-second blast; — = four- to six-second blast)

INTERNATIONAL (ACTION BEING TAKEN)		INLAND (ACTION PROPOSED TO BE TAKEN)	
MEETING OR CROSSING AND ACTION IS REQUIRED (NO ANSWER REQUIRED):		MEETING OR CROSSING WITHIN ½ MILE OF EACH OTHER AND ACTION IS REQUIRED (AGREEMENT BY SAME SIGNAL REQUIRED):	
I am altering course to starboard	•	*I propose leaving you to port*	•
I am altering course to port	• •	*I propose leaving you to starboard*	• •
I am operating astern propulsion	• • •	*I am operating astern propulsion*	• • •
OVERTAKING IN A NARROW CHANNEL OR FAIRWAY AND ACTION IS REQUIRED (AGREEMENT REQUIRED BEFORE ACTION):		OVERTAKING IN A NARROW CHANNEL OR FAIRWAY AND ACTION IS REQUIRED (AGREEMENT BY SAME SIGNAL REQUIRED BEFORE ACTION):	
I intend to overtake on your starboard	— — •	*I propose overtaking on your starboard*	•
I intend to overtake on your port	— — • •	*I propose overtaking on your port*	• •
I agree to be overtaken	— • — •	*I agree to be overtaken*	• *or* • •
Warning—I don't understand your intentions	• • • • •	*Warning—I don't understand your intentions*	• • • • •
Approaching a bend in a channel	—	*Approaching a bend in a channel or leaving berth or dock*	—

Vessels are also required to make sound signals when in or near areas of restricted visibility. These signals, identical for both International and Inland Rules, are shown below.

Sound Signals in Restricted Visibility

(• = one-second blast; — = four- to six-second blast. Repeat every two minutes, maximum.)

Power vessel making way	—
Power vessel stopped	— —
Manned tow	— • • •
Pilot vessel—optional	• • • •

Not under command, restricted in ability to maneuver, constrained by draft, sailing, fishing, towing or pushing, fishing at anchor, restricted at anchor — • •

ANCHORED:

Less than 100 meters—ring bell rapidly for five seconds every minute

Greater than or equal to 100 meters—ring bell five seconds fore, then gong five seconds aft

Additional option • — •

AGROUND:

three distinct claps of bell + rapid five-second bell + three claps, all repeated at one minute

Vessel less than twelve meters option—any sound at two minutes

Lights—What Can They Tell You?

Definitions

RULES

21-22

The Rules specify the colors and arcs of visibility of navigation lights to be carried by each type of vessel, as shown at right:

Masthead light (also known as steaming light): white light on centerline showing forward from 22.5° abaft the beam on either side (225° arc).

Sidelights: green on starboard and red on port, each visible from dead ahead to 22.5° abaft the beam. On vessels less than twenty meters, the sidelights may be combined in one unit on the centerline.

Sternlight: white light at stern showing aft from 22.5° abaft the beam on either side (135° arc).

Towing light: the same as a sternlight, except for being yellow.

All-around light: a light of any color that shows 360° around.

Flashing light: a light flashing at a minimum of 120 times per minute.

Special flashing light (Inland): a light flashing at fifty-seventy times per minute over an arc of 180–225°.

Range of Visibility

The Rules also specify minimum ranges of visibility under clear conditions for navigation lights. The table at right shows these ranges according to the size of the boat. Note that, in addition to the information specified in this table, inconspicuous, partly submerged vessels or objects being towed should carry a white all-around light, visible at a distance of three miles.

Color Presentation

Color illustrations of required navigation-light groupings for various vessels follow on pages 33–40.

Rules 21–22: Colors and Areas of Visibility

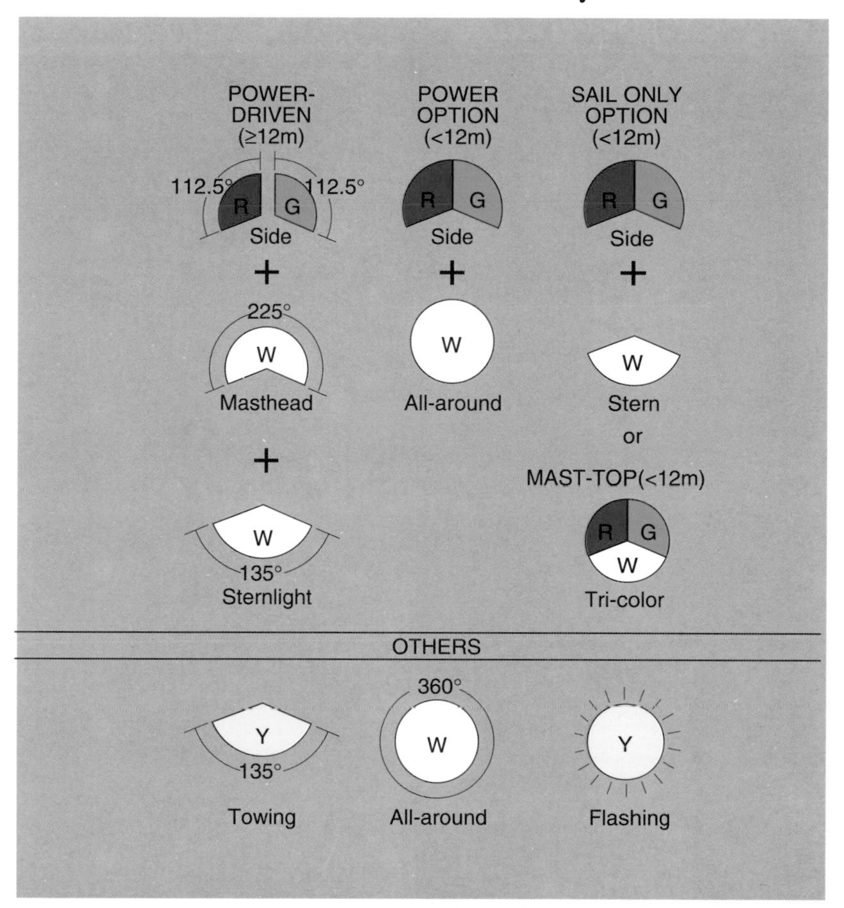

Type of Light	Vessel Length in meters	Visibility in miles
MASTHEAD	under 12	2
	12–20	3
	20–50	5
	over 50	6
SIDE	under 12	1
	12–50	2
	over 50	3
STERN, TOWING, AND ALL-AROUND	under 50	2
	over 50	3

Rule 30: Anchored Vessels and Vessels Aground

VESSEL	GROUPS	SHAPES	VIEW FROM SIDE	BOW	STERN
Anchored ≥7 m <50 m	All-round (1)				
Anchored 50–100 m	All-round (2)				
Anchored ≥100 m	All-round (2) All deck lights				
Aground <50 m	All-round (1) R/R				
Aground ≥50 m	All-round (2) R/R				

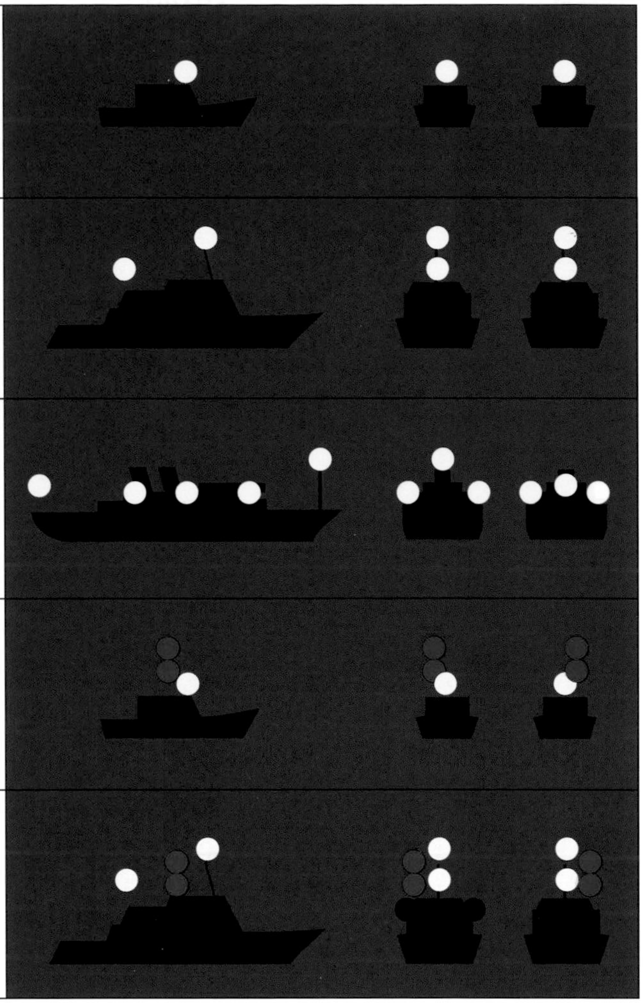

Rule 31: Seaplanes

VESSEL	GROUPS	SHAPES	VIEW FROM SIDE	BOW	STERN
Seaplane Underway	Masthead Side Stern	None			

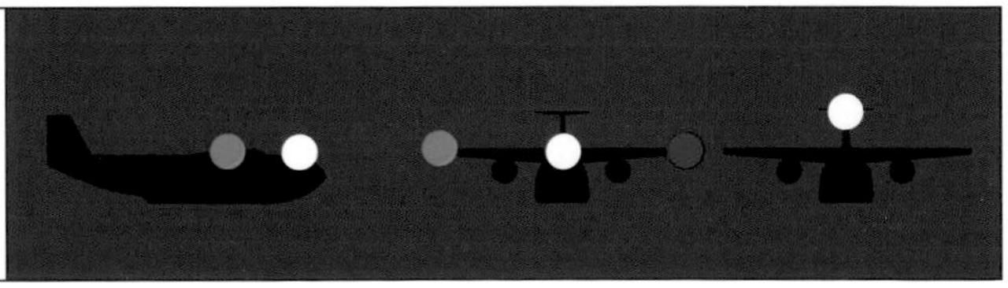

VHF Radio

Most recreational boaters use the VHF radio to:

- chitchat with their boating friends
- arrange for fuel and docking
- listen to marine weather forecasts
- call for help when they break down

Strangely, few use it for its primary intended purpose—communication with other vessels regarding safe navigation. The Vessel Bridge-to-Bridge Radiotelephone Act requires certain vessels to monitor CH13 when underway within the three mile limit. These are:

- power-driven vessels over twenty meters
- inspected passenger vessels over 100 tons
- towing vessels over twenty-six feet
- dredges

In addition, the U.S. Coast Guard has established Security Broadcast Systems in most large coastal ports. In these systems, vessels required to monitor CH13 are also requested to report their movements fifteen minutes prior to getting underway, upon getting underway, and at certain check points in entering and leaving the port.

CH13 is thus your best source of information regarding the movements of large vessels in Inland waters. When you have a question regarding the intentions of another vessel—whether in a head-on, crossing, or overtaking situation—call the vessel first on CH13. If you get no response on CH13, try CH16.

A few ports, as well as traffic separation schemes and vessel traffic services, operate on channels other than CH13—usually CH11, CH12, or CH14. Consult the *U.S. Coast Pilot*, or call the nearest Coast Guard station on CH16 to obtain the channel for a specific area.

While the International Rules do not allow for the use of VHF radio in lieu of whistle signals, it has become common practice among large ships to exchange navigational information on CH16.

When contacting another vessel on VHF, keep in mind the area your signal will cover. CH13 is restricted to one watt, giving it an effective range of about five miles. The limit for CH16 is twenty-five watts, giving it a range of twenty or more miles. On CH13, you will be heard by every boat within eighty square miles; on CH16, you will be heard over at least one thousand square miles. Therefore, when attempting to contact an unknown vessel, be as specific as possible. Do not say, “I am calling the sailboat one mile on my port bow.” The listener is not on your vessel, so he has no idea where your port bow is! Better to say, “I am calling a northerly-bound vessel. Captain, I am the fifty-foot white power vessel one mile on your starboard quarter.” Now the listener knows exactly where to look to see if he is the one being hailed.

SECTION 2

International and Inland Rules

PART A: General

Rule 1: Application

What It Says

The italicized text indicates where the Inland Rules differ substantially from the COLREGS.

(a) These Rules shall apply to all vessels upon the high seas and in all waters connected therewith navigable by seagoing vessels. *These Rules apply to all vessels upon the inland waters of the United States, and to vessels of the United States on the Canadian waters of the Great Lakes to the extent that there is no conflict with Canadian law.*

(b) Nothing in these Rules shall interfere with the operation of special rules made by an appropriate authority for roadsteads, harbors, rivers, lakes or inland waterways connected with the high seas and navigable by seagoing vessels. Such special rules shall conform as closely as possible to these Rules.

(b) (i) These Rules constitute special rules made by an appropriate authority within the meaning of Rule 1 (b) of the International Regulations.

(ii) All vessels complying with the construction and equipment requirements of the International Regulations are considered to be in compliance with these Rules.

RULE

1

Application

(c) Nothing in these Rules shall interfere with the operation of any special rules made by the Government of any State *(the Secretary of the Navy)* with respect to additional station or signal lights, shapes or whistle signals for ships of war and vessels proceeding under convoy, with respect to additional station or signal lights or shapes for fishing vessels engaged in fishing as a fleet. These additional station or signal lights, shapes or whistle signals shall, so far as possible, be such that they cannot be mistaken for any light, shape or signal authorized elsewhere under these Rules.[1] *Notice of such special rules shall be published in the Federal Register and, after the effective date specified in such notice, they shall have effect as if they were a part of these Rules.*[1]

(d) Traffic separation schemes may be adopted by the Organization for the purpose of these Rules. *Traffic separation schemes may be established for the purposes of these rules. Vessel traffic service regulations may be in effect in certain areas.*

(e) Whenever the Government *(Secretary)* concerned shall have determined that a vessel *(or class)* of special construction or purpose cannot comply fully with the provisions of any of these Rules with respect to the number, position, range or arc of visibility of lights or shapes, as well as to the disposition and characteristics of sound-signalling appliances, without interfering with the special function of the vessel, such vessel shall comply with such other provisions in regard to the number, position, range or arc of visibility of lights or shapes, as well as to the disposition and characteristics of sound signalling appliances, as her Government *(the Secretary)* shall have determined to be the closest possible compliance with these Rules in respect to that vessel. *The Secretary may issue a certificate of alternative compliance for a vessel or class of vessels specifying the closest possible compliance with these Rules. The Secretary of the navy shall make these determinations and issue certificates of alternative compliance for vessels of the Navy.*

(f) The Secretary may accept a certificate of alternative compliance issued by a contracting party to the International Regulations if he determines that the alternative compliance standards of the contracting party are substantially the same as those of the United States.

[1] Submarines may display, as a distinctive means of identification, an intermittent flashing amber (yellow) beacon with a sequence of operation of one flash per second for three (3) seconds followed by a three (3) second off-period. Other special rules made by the Secretary of the Navy with respect to additional station and signal lights are found in Part 707 of Title 32, Code of Federal Regulations (32 CFR 707).

What It Means

The International Rules (COLREGS) apply to all of the oceans and bodies of water connected to them. In the U. S., the "special rules" consist of the United States Inland Rules, applicable to the Great Lakes, Western Rivers, waterways, and specific bays inside the magenta COLREGS Demarcation Line printed on charts.

Some boaters think that the International Rules apply uniformly to any waters beyond three miles from land. The actual demarcation lines between the International and Inland Rules are listed in the back of the official *Navigation Rules: International—Inland*. There you will find that, with the exception of Casco Bay, the entire Coast of Maine, including its numerous deep bays, is subject to the International Rules. Similarly, Puget Sound on the West Coast falls under the International Rules. Study the demarcation lines in your area so that you will always know which rules apply.

Boats fishing as a fleet and warships may employ unique lights, shapes, and sound signals, as long as they cannot be confused with ones specified in the International Rules. Annex 2 of both the International and the Inland Rules, specifies the unique lights for trawlers and purse seiners fishing in close proximity. For example, purse seiners may show two yellow lights in a vertical line, flashing alternately every second, with equal on-off periods.

Traffic separation schemes are found in busy areas such as approaches to major harbors. They consist of one or more parallel pairs of inbound and outbound traffic lanes, each pair separated by a separation line or zone. The lanes and their termination points are clearly marked in magenta (red) on NOAA charts.

Boats of unusual construction or purpose may have noncomplying lights and sound-signals, as long as they do comply as closely as possible to the specifications in the rules. A submarine, for example, may have a forward steaming light lower than its sidelights, because it has no forward mast on which to mount the light.

Responsibility

Rule 2: Responsibility

What It Says

(a) Nothing in these Rules shall exonerate any vessel, or the owner, master or crew thereof, from the consequences of any neglect to comply with these Rules or of the neglect of any precaution which may be required by the ordinary practice of seamen, or by the special circumstances of the case.

(b) In construing and complying with these Rules due regard shall be had to all dangers of navigation and collision and to any special circumstances, including the limitations of the vessels involved, which may make a departure from these Rules necessary to avoid immediate danger.

What It Means

Rule 2 is the most important of the Rules. It charges that, no matter what happens, the person in charge of the vessel must do everything possible to avoid collision. In avoiding collision, you must consider your own vessel's maneuvering characteristics, the maneuvering characteristics of the other vessel, and any other hazards to navigation that may affect your decisions.

Rule 2 also says that you are allowed, and in some instances expected, to break the Rules when danger of collision is immediate. Departure from the Rules might be required, for example, by shallow water, a ledge or other obstruction, or the presence of other vessels.

In general, the Rules are designed to avoid collision between two vessels, not three or more. In a situation involving many vessels in a small area, you are forced to substitute common sense and good manners for the Rules. Rule 2 gives you permission.

In summary, Rule 2 removes any argument that a participant in a collision is without fault.

Rule 3: General Definitions

What It Says

For the purpose of these Rules *(and this Act)*, except where the context otherwise requires:

(a) The word "Vessel" includes every description of water craft, including nondisplacement craft and seaplanes, used or capable of being used as a means of transportation on water.

(b) The term "Power-driven vessel" means any vessel propelled by machinery.

(c) The term "Sailing vessel" means any vessel under sail provided that propelling machinery, if fitted, is not being used.

(d) The term "Vessel engaged in fishing" means any vessel fishing with nets, lines, trawls or other fishing apparatus which restrict maneuverability, but does not include a vessel fishing with trolling lines or other fishing apparatus which do not restrict maneuverability.

(e) The word "Seaplane" includes any aircraft designed to maneuver on the water.

(f) The term "Vessel not under command" means a vessel which through some exceptional circumstance is unable to maneuver as required by these Rules and is therefore unable to keep out of the way of another vessel.

(g) The term "Vessel restricted in her ability to maneuver" means a vessel which from the nature of her work is restricted in her ability to maneuver as required by these Rules and is therefore unable to keep out of the way of another vessel. The term "Vessels restricted in their ability to maneuver" shall include but not be limited to:

(i) a vessel engaged in laying, servicing or picking up a navigation mark, submarine cable or pipeline;

(ii) a vessel engaged in dredging, surveying or underwater operations;

(iii) a vessel engaged in replenishment or transferring persons, provisions or cargo while underway;

(iv) a vessel engaged in the launching or recovery of aircraft;

(v) a vessel engaged in mine clearance operations;

(vi) a vessel engaged in a towing operation such as severely restricts the towing vessel and her tow in their ability to deviate from their course.

(h) The term "Vessel constrained by her draft" means a power-driven vessel which, because of her draft in relation to the available depth and width of navigable water is severely restricted in her ability to deviate from the course she is following.

RULE

3

General Definitions

Note that there is no mention of a "Vessel constrained by her draft" anywhere in the Inland Rules.

(i) The word "underway" means that a vessel is not at anchor, or made fast to the shore, or aground.

(j) The words "length" and "breadth" of a vessel means her length overall and greatest breadth.

(k) Vessels shall be deemed to be in sight of one another only when one can be observed visually from the other.

(l) The term "restricted visibility" means any condition in which visibility is restricted by fog, mist, falling snow, heavy rainstorms, sandstorms or any other similar causes.

(l) "Western Rivers" means the Mississippi River, its tributaries, South Pass, and Southwest Pass, to the navigational demarcation lines dividing the high seas from harbors, rivers, and other inland waters of the United States, and the Port Allen-Morgan City Alternate Route, and that part of the Atchafalaya River above its junction with the Port Allen-Morgan City Alternate Route including the Old River and the Red River;

(m) "Great Lakes" means the Great Lakes and their connecting and tributary waters including the Calumet River as far as the Thomas J. O'Brien Lock and Controlling Works (between mile 326 and 327), the Chicago River as far as the east side of the Ashland Avenue Bridge (between mile 321 and 322), and the Saint Lawrence River as far east as the lower exit of Saint Lambert Lock;

(n) "Secretary" means the Secretary of the department in which the Coast Guard is operating;

(o) "Inland Waters" means the navigable waters of the United States shoreward of the navigational demarcation lines dividing the high seas from harbors, rivers, and other inland waters of the United States and the waters of the Great Lakes on the United States side of the International Boundary;

(p) "Inland Rules" or "Rules" mean the Inland Navigational Rules and the annexes thereto, which govern the conduct of vessels and specify the lights, shapes, and sound signals that apply on inland waters; and

(q) "International Regulations" means the International Regulations for Preventing Collisions at Sea, 1972, including annexes currently in force for the United States.

What It Means

Definitions

Vessel: Anything capable of being used for transport on water. A bathtub, a log, even Herbie "the Lovebug," can all be vessels.

Power-driven vessel: Any vessel using an engine for propulsion.

Sailing vessel: Sailboat under sail, not using an engine for propulsion. With engine engaged it becomes, by definition, a "power-driven vessel."

Vessel engaged in fishing: Boat using fishing equipment that limits its maneuverability (nets, trawls, etc.). A sport-fishing, angling, or trolling boat is not a "vessel engaged in fishing" for the purposes of the Rules. A lobster or crab boat might be when it is hauling or setting traps. The key issue is the degree to which the fishing apparatus limits maneuverability. If you are sport fishing, don't take a chance.

Vessel not under command: Not "without a person in command," but rather a vessel that, due to accident, breakdown, or other circumstance, is unable to alter course or speed in order to avoid collision. Examples include boats whose engines or steering mechanisms have broken, boats dragging anchor, or becalmed sailboats with no auxiliary engine.

Vessel restricted in her ability to maneuver: Activities that specifically restrict ability to maneuver include: buoy tending, laying cable or pipe, dredging, surveying, diving, transferring materials underway, launching or recovering aircraft, minesweeping, and towing. The terminology, "vessel engaged in a towing operation such as severely restricts the towing vessel and her tow in their ability to deviate from their course," raises the question of the definition of the word "severely." Courtesy and caution dictate that you include any boat involved in towing.

Vessel constrained by her draft: Vessels having especially deep draft relative to the depth of water are allowed to claim special status under the International Rules. *There is no mention of a "vessel constrained by her draft" anywhere in the Inland Rules, no doubt because in inland waters, every boat would qualify.*

Underway: Not necessarily making way (moving relative to the water), but simply not anchored, grounded, or otherwise attached to shore. A "vessel at anchor" is one whose anchor is on the bottom and holding. A vessel dragging her anchor has at times been judged underway, at other times a "vessel not under command."

Length and breadth: Maximum or overall length, and maximum width.

RULES

4 & 5

Application/ Lookout

PART B: Steering and Sailing Rules

SECTION 1 CONDUCT OF VESSELS IN ANY CONDITION OF VISIBILITY

Rule 4: Application

What It Says

Rules in this Section apply to any condition of visibility.

Rule 5: Lookout

What It Says

Every vessel shall at all times maintain a proper lookout by sight and hearing as well as by all available means appropriate in the prevailing circumstances and conditions so as to make a full appraisal of the situation and of the risk of collision.

The italicized text indicates where the Inland Rules differ substantially from the COLREGS.

What They Mean

In over half of all marine accident hearings, both vessels involved in collision have been charged with failure to maintain an effective lookout.

In the case of the freighter *TFL Express,* which ran down the single-handed sailboat, *Granholm* (see page 13), the court assigned equal blame, saying, "The obligation to maintain a proper lookout falls upon great vessels and small alike."

In the case of the bulk carrier *Sealnes* running down the dive-tender *Mr. Fission* (page 22), the *Sealnes* essentially relied on Vancouver vessel traffic services to maintain the lookout for them. The skipper of *Mr. Fission,* acting as owner, captain, and sidewalk superintendant of engine repairs, certainly failed to "at all times maintain a proper lookout."

It has been ruled that requiring a single individual to steer, navigate, and keep the lookout all at the same time is improper. The intent of the law is that the lookout devote his or her entire attention to the job of looking for other boats.

Further, it has been ruled that, considering limited visibility in fog and engine noise, a "proper lookout by sight and hearing" for any but the smallest of boats is one stationed at the bow, not at the helm. Communication between the helm and the lookout can be by intercom, or handheld VHF, if necessary.

What about a single-hander who inevitably must get some sleep? The court has ruled that failure of a single-hander to maintain a proper—i.e., constant—lookout, in spite of the need to sleep, is irresponsible in the sense of Rule 2. In other words, long, single-handed passages are themselves irresponsible.

"All available means" includes not only eyeballs and ears, but binoculars, radar, and VHF radio, as well. Obviously, radar should be used in fog, rain, and snow. But it should also be used at night, due to the possibility of unlit objects or vessels in your path. It has even been ruled that radar should be employed in clear daylight conditions, because of its unparalleled ability to measure range and bearing to targets.

Radar supplements, but does not replace, a visual lookout. Small wooden and fiberglass boats may be undetectable by radar beyond a fraction of a mile. With the radar on a long-range setting, close targets can be lost in the clutter. On the other hand, setting the radar to a short range may show close targets, but not potentially dangerous and fast-moving targets beyond the range, and it doesn't allow a sense of the overall traffic situation.

Vessels of 300 tons, passenger vessels of 100 tons, tow boats of twenty-six feet, and dredges working in or near channels are all required to communicate on VHF Channel 13. Vessels using traffic separation schemes and vessel traffic services also use designated VHF channels. Find out what these channels are, either by calling the Coast Guard or by consulting a Coast Pilot, and monitor them when in their areas.

RULE

6

Safe Speed

Rule 6: Safe Speed

What It Says

Every vessel shall at all times proceed at a safe speed so that she can take proper and effective action to avoid collision and be stopped within a distance appropriate to the prevailing circumstances and conditions. In determining a safe speed the following factors shall be among those taken into account:

(a) By all vessels:

(i) the state of visibility;

(ii) the traffic density including concentrations of fishing vessels or any other vessels;

(iii) the maneuverability of the vessel with special reference to stopping distance and turning ability in the prevailing conditions;

(iv) at night the presence of background light such as from shore lights or from back scatter of her own lights;

(v) the state of wind, sea and current, and the proximity of navigational hazards;

(vi) the draft in relation to the available depth of water.

(b) Additionally, by vessels with operational radar:

(i) the characteristics, efficiency and limitations of the radar equipment;

(ii) any constraints imposed by the radar range scale in use;

(iii) the effect on radar detection of the sea state, weather and other sources of interference;

(iv) the possibility that small vessels, ice and other floating objects may not be detected by radar at an adequate range;

(v) the number, location and movement of vessels detected by radar;

(vi) the more exact assessment of the visibility that may be possible when radar is used to determine the range of vessels or other objects in the vicinity.

What It Means

Like automobiles, boats are required to limit their speed in order to be able to avoid collision. Factors determining safe speed include:

- visibility conditions
- background lights
- traffic intensity
- maneuverability
- wind and current
- navigational hazards
- depth of water
- the limitations of radar

How do you define "safe speed"? More than once, courts have applied as a rule of thumb "that speed which would allow stopping within half the range of visibility." Even this definition fails, however, when the hazards are below the surface. The atmospheric "visibility" was excellent on the night the Titanic struck the iceberg.

Note that the Rules do not define safe speed in so many words. Instead, the Rules tell you to constantly evaluate prevailing circumstances and conditions. Safe speed well outside a fog bank might be ten knots; safe speed within the fog might be only two knots; safe speed as you approach the fog bank would also be just a few knots, since you don't know what is headed toward you from inside it.

Rule 6 lists factors to be taken into account. The phrase "among those" means that the list is not to be considered complete. There is no way to predict what other special circumstances the prudent mariner should take into account in judging the safe speed for his boat.

Rule 6 also lists a number of additional factors to be considered by boats having radar. This list is likewise incomplete. Obviously, radar is an aid that tends to increase safe speed. Due to the limitations of radar and the limited reflectivity of some targets, however, it would be foolish to equate safe speed using radar to safe speed with unlimited visibility.

Mast-mounted radars on sailboats suffer from blind sectors of a few degrees. A wise precaution for the sailor is to periodically alter course five–ten degrees for a few sweeps of the radar, in order to see what's lurking or coming up in the blind sector.

RULE

6

Safe Speed

The limitations of radar ranges were mentioned previously under Rule 5, Lookout. Good seamanship would include changing the range of the radar periodically in order to keep track of both the long-range situation and the weaker, close-in targets.

Both waves and precipitation return radar echoes. Since these are not of interest, they are considered to be noise or clutter. Radar sets are equipped with "clutter" controls to reduce (sea) wave and rain echoes, and should be used to produce the best discrimination under the circumstances. Clutter is reduced, however, by simply reducing overall sensitivity within a certain range, and should thus be taken into account when judging safe speed.

Safe speed is not necessarily zero speed. A boat dead in the water has no steerage and, therefore, no ability to change course to avoid collision. In particular, Rule 19(e) states that, under conditions of restricted visibility, a vessel that hears another vessel forward of her beam "shall reduce her speed to the minimum at which she can be kept on her course," i.e., to bare steerageway and "if necessary, take all her way off."

In spite of the fact that courts have repeatedly ruled "safe speed" to mean a speed that would allow a vessel to stop in one-half of its range of visibility, commercial vessels routinely operate at nearly top speed in conditions where they can barely see their own bows. The reasons are numerous: the pressure to maintain schedules; the illusion that radar is an infallible device; and a false sense of confidence that increases with each uneventful passage through fog.

The potential consequences of breaking Rule 6 are unimaginable. After losing the *Andrea Doria,* while operating at full speed in fog, her captain was heard to moan, " When I was a boy, and all my life, I loved the sea; now I hate it."

Rule 7: Risk of Collision

What It Says

(a) Every vessel shall use all available means appropriate to the prevailing circumstances and conditions to determine if risk of collision exists. If there is any doubt such risk shall be deemed to exist.
(b) Proper use shall be made of radar equipment if fitted and operational, including long-range scanning to obtain early warning of risk of collision and radar plotting or equivalent systematic observation of detected objects.
(c) Assumptions shall not be made on the basis of scanty information, especially scanty radar information.
(d) In determining if risk of collision exists the following considerations shall be among those taken into account:

(i) such risk shall be deemed to exist if the compass heading of an approaching vessel does not appreciably change;
(ii) such risk may sometimes exist even when an appreciable bearing change is evident, particularly when approaching a very large vessel or a tow or when approaching a vessel at close range.

What It Means

You must use all available means to determine if collision with another boat is possible (not "likely," but "possible"). Collision is possible if the compass bearing (or relative bearing at steady course and speed) remains constant. If there is any doubt, you must assume collision is possible and act well in advance!

"All available means" to assess the risk of collision obviously includes the taking and plotting of compass bearings in clear visibility and the use of radar to track bearings in conditions of limited visibility. Considering the ease of tracking relative bearings on even the least expensive small-boat radar, it is safe to assume that the use of radar under clear conditions would also be expected.

The warning "assumptions shall not be made on the basis of scanty information" relates mostly to the difficulty of taking accurate bearings. At long range, bearing errors of several degrees could produce opposing predictions of crossing ahead or crossing behind. If a

(continued)

Risk of Collision

boat is pitching or rolling, compass bearings can easily be five or more degrees in error.

Relative bearing (bearing relative to your boat's heading) is often used instead of compass bearing when using radar. Relative bearings are valid only if both heading and speed of the boat taking the bearing are constant, however.

Similarly, relative bearings taken by lining a target up against parts of your own boat (such as a stanchion) are only valid with constant speed and heading and a constant position of your eye!

You can use VHF radio to clarify another boat's intentions. But VHF has its limitations, chiefly the difficulty of determining the name of the boat you want to contact. A call to "the boat off Snug Harbor proceeding north," could raise several responses. To assume you have reached the intended boat might prove very dangerous. Better to state, "calling the trawler off Snug Harbor proceeding north. I am the overtaking white forty-foot sailboat one-half mile off your starboard quarter."

Never assume that a boat whose course seems unthreatening won't suddenly change it, thereby presenting a risk of collision. This is especially true at night and in fog, when the other boat might not even be aware of you. Assessing risk of collision is a full-time job.

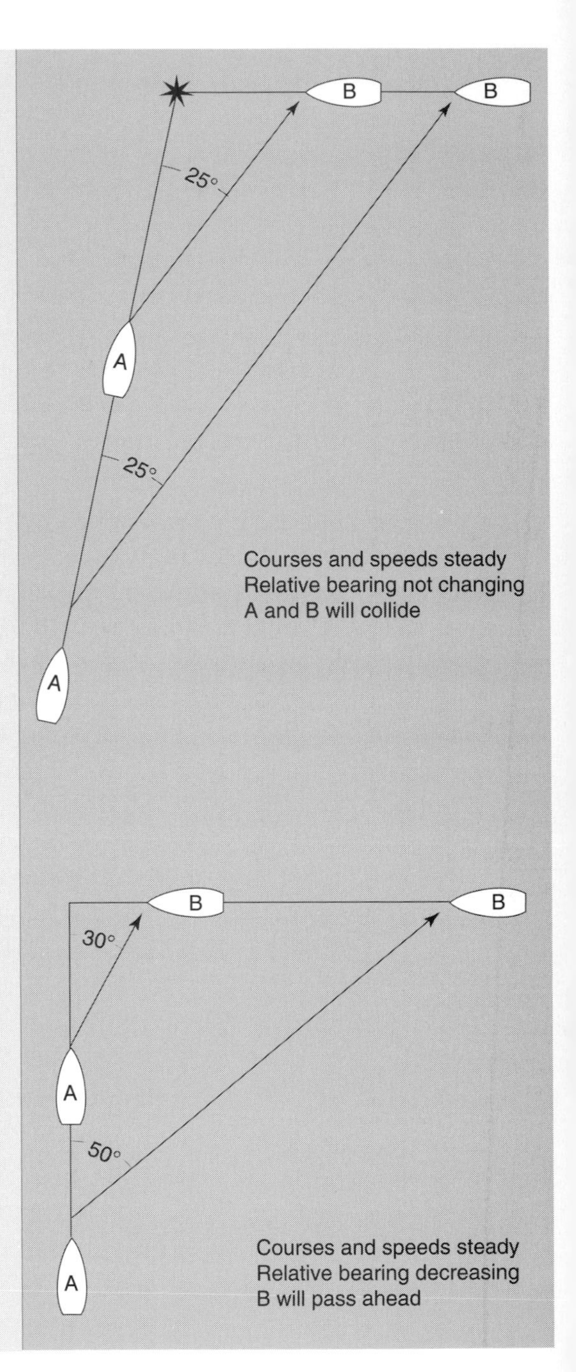

As you can see from the story on page 16, the *Andrea Doria* ignored nearly every part of Rule 7:

(a) She failed to establish the identity and nature of the target first observed at seventeen miles, and, though there was certainly doubt as to whether risk of collision existed, she failed to assume its existence.

(b) Although she had a very accurate radar device, she failed to plot the course of the target in order to determine risk of collision.

(c) She assumed the other vessel to be a fishing vessel (and, therefore, assumed the vessel to be small and slow).

Rule 8: Action to Avoid Collision

What It Says

(a) Any action taken to avoid collision shall, if the circumstances of the case admit, be positive, made in ample time and with due regard to the observance of good seamanship.

(b) Any alteration of course and/or speed to avoid collision shall, if the circumstances of the case admit, be large enough to be readily apparent to another vessel observing visually or by radar; a succession of small alterations of course and/or speed should be avoided.

(c) If there is sufficient sea room, alteration of course alone may be the most effective action to avoid a close-quarters situation provided that it is made in good time, is substantial and does not result in another close-quarters situation.

(d) Action taken to avoid collision with another vessel shall be such as to result in passing at a safe distance. The effectiveness of the action shall be carefully checked until the other vessel is finally past and clear.

(e) If necessary to avoid collision or allow more time to assess the situation, a vessel shall slacken her speed or take all way off by stopping or reversing her means of propulsion.

(f) (i) A vessel which, by any of these rules, is required not to impede the passage or safe passage of another vessel shall, when required by the circumstances of the case, take early action to allow sufficient sea room for the safe passage of the other vessel.
(ii) A vessel required not to impede the passage or safe passage of another vessel is not relieved of this obligation if approaching the other vessel so as to involve risk of collision and shall, when taking action, have full regard to the action which may be required by the rules of this part.
(iii) A vessel, the passage of which is not to be impeded remains fully obliged to comply with the rules of this part when the two vessels are approaching one another so as to involve risk of collision.

What It Means

Stress is placed on the fact that a give-way vessel must take significant and obvious action in ample time (before the stand-on vessel begins to question your intent). The alteration of course or speed must be large enough to be obvious to the other boat. At night, for example, the change of course should be large enough to show a different navigation light. Never make a series of small changes.

Given enough room, alterations to course are usually preferable to alterations in speed because course changes are more apparent from the other boat. Again, at night, the course change in a meeting or crossing situation should be large enough to display your opposite bow light; i.e., swing your bow past the stand-on boat.

On the other hand, a dramatic change in speed is acceptable if the stand-on boat is approaching you from your beam. In such a case, slowing down would be better than speeding up for several reasons:

a) Rule 15 states, "When two power-driven vessels are crossing so as to involve risk of collision, the vessel which has the other on her own starboard shall keep out of the way and shall, if the circumstances of the case admit, avoid crossing ahead of the other vessel."
b) Power boats usually travel at close to maximum speed anyway.
c) If a collision did occur, damage would be less at low speed than at high speed.

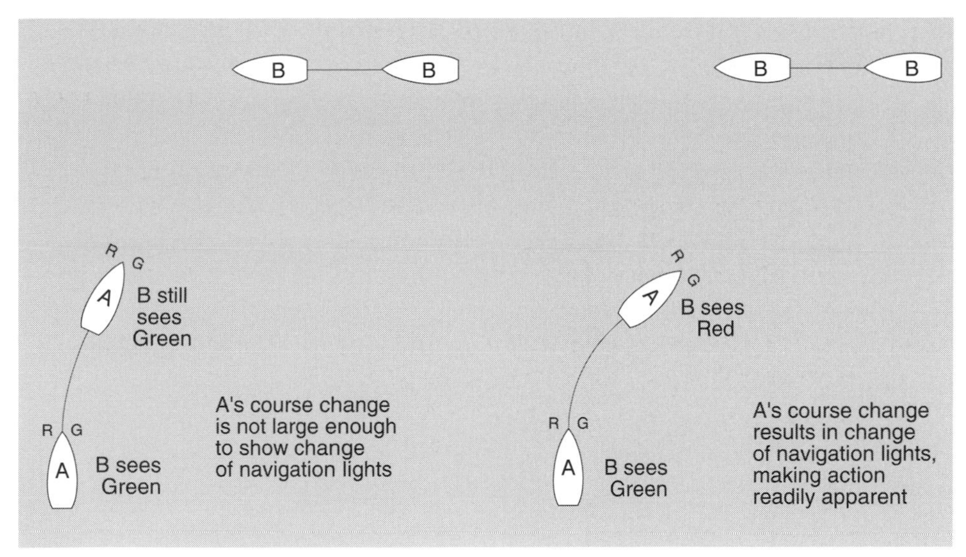

Action to Avoid Collision

Rule 9: Narrow Channels

What It Says

(a) *(i)* A vessel proceeding along the course of a narrow channel or fairway shall keep as near to the outer limit of the channel or fairway which lies on her starboard side as is safe and practicable.

(ii) Notwithstanding paragraph (a)(i) and Rule 14(a), a power-driven vessel operating in narrow channels or fairways on the Great Lakes, Western Rivers, or waters specified by the Secretary, and proceeding downbound with a following current shall have the right-of-way over an upbound vessel, shall propose the manner and place of passage, and shall initiate the maneuvering signals prescribed by rule 34(a)(i), as appropriate. The vessel proceeding upbound against the current shall hold as necessary to permit safe passing.

(b) A vessel of less than 20 meters in length or a sailing vessel shall not impede the passage of a vessel which can safely navigate only within a narrow channel or fairway.

(c) A vessel engaged in fishing shall not impede the passage of any other vessel navigating within a narrow channel or fairway.

(d) A vessel shall not cross a narrow channel or fairway if such crossing impedes the passage of a vessel which can safely navigate only within such channel or fairway. The latter vessel may *(shall)* use the sound signal prescribed in Rule 34(d) if in doubt as to the intention of the crossing vessel.

(e) (i) In a narrow channel or fairway when overtaking can take place only if the vessel to be overtaken has to take action to permit safe passing*, the vessel intending to overtake shall indicate her intention by sounding the appropriate signal prescribed in Rule 34(c)(i). The vessel to be overtaken shall, if in agreement, sound the appropriate signal prescribed in Rule 34(c)(ii) and take steps to permit safe passing. If in doubt she may sound the signals prescribed in Rule 34(d).

(ii) This Rule does not relieve the overtaking vessel of her obligation under Rule 13.

(f) A vessel nearing a bend or an area of a narrow channel or fairway where other vessels may be obscured by an intervening obstruction shall navigate with particular alertness and caution and shall sound the appropriate signal prescribed in Rule 34(e).

(g) Any vessel shall, if the circumstances of the case admit, avoid anchoring in a narrow channel.

* *Note that the Inland Rules require the overtaking vessel to give a sound signal regardless of whether action by the overtaken vessel is required.*

What It Means

"Narrow channel" is not defined in the Rules. There are no limits to width, length, or depth of a narrow channel, except in relation to the boats involved. Generally, a channel may be considered narrow when, due to depth or distance between hazards, one or both boats are severely limited in room to maneuver. A channel marked by buoys may be considered a narrow channel by a deep draft boat, but not by a shallower draft boat that could navigate outside of the buoys.

Boats proceeding along narrow channels are required to stay, not just to the right of the centerline, but "as near to the outer limit of the channel or fairway that lies on her starboard side as is safe and practicable." Thus, smaller, shallower-draft boats should stay further to the right than larger, deeper-draft boats facilitating the passing of the larger, faster boats. You are also expected to remain on the starboard side, not just when encountering other boats but at all times.

Note that the Inland Rules differ on this point, stating that *"a downbound boat has the right-of-way over an upbound boat and should propose the manner of passing with the maneuvering signals in Rule 34."*

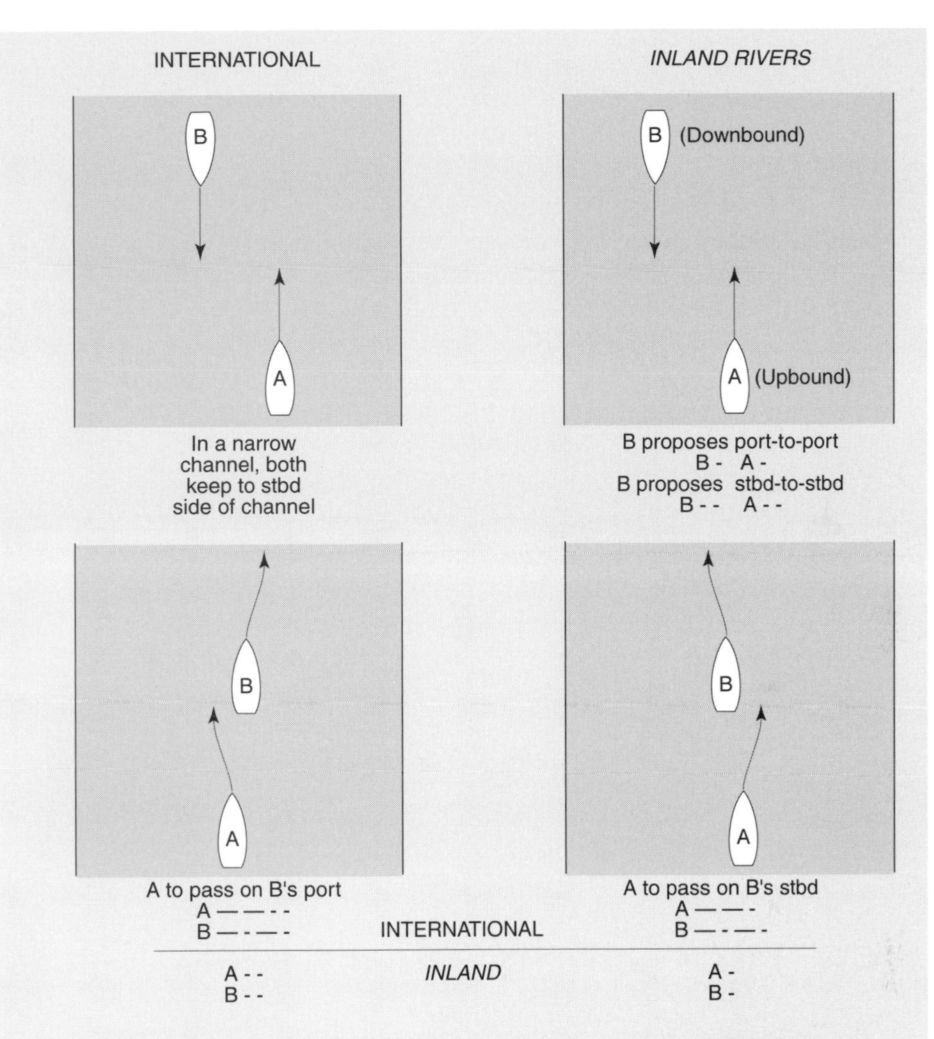

If a sailboat in a narrow channel cannot stay close to the starboard edge because she is tacking against the wind, she still must not impede a boat that can safely navigate only within the narrow channel or fairway.

Fishing is not prohibited in a narrow channel, but a fishing boat must get out of the way of any other boat (not only a "vessel constrained by draft") that is using the channel.

You must not cross a narrow channel if your crossing will impede the passage of another boat that is constrained to the channel. Rule 9(d) does not prohibit crossing narrow channels at other times, nor does it override The Crossing Rule (Rule 15) for boats that are not constrained to the channel.

Under International Rules, when a boat being overtaken has to do anything but maintain course and speed to be safely passed, the boats must exchange the signals of Rule 34. Under Inland Rules, however, a vessel intending to overtake another vessel in a narrow channel must initiate the signals of Rule 34, regardless of whether maneuvering is required of the overtaken vessel. When signals are given, the overtaking boat can only proceed after the overtaken boat has signaled agreement. If the overtaken boat does not agree, she must sound the danger signal. At this point, communication by VHF radio is in order before taking further action.

Boats approaching a bend or other blind area must sound one prolonged blast. Boats approaching in opposite directions and hearing the blast should respond in kind. Navigating "with particular alertness and caution" includes not cutting the corner when you can't see what is around the bend and allowing a vessel that is proceeding with the current to go first.

Rule 10: Traffic Separation Schemes

What It Says

(a) This Rule applies to traffic separation schemes adopted by the Organization and does not relieve any vessel of her obligation under any other rule.

(b) A vessel using a traffic separation scheme shall:

(i) proceed in the appropriate traffic lane in the general direction of traffic flow for that lane;

(ii) so far as practicable keep clear of a traffic separation line or separation zone;

(iii) normally join or leave a traffic lane at the termination of the lane, but when joining or leaving from either side shall do so at as small an angle to the general direction of traffic flow as practicable.

(c) A vessel shall, so far as practicable, avoid crossing traffic lanes but if obliged to do so shall cross on a heading as nearly as practicable at right angles to the general direction of traffic flow.

(d) (i) A vessel shall not use an inshore traffic zone when she can safely use the appropriate traffic lane within the adjacent traffic separation scheme. However, vessels of less than 20 meters in length, sailing vessels and vessels engaged in fishing may use the inshore traffic zone.

(ii) Notwithstanding subparagraph (d)(i), a vessel may use an inshore traffic zone when en route to or from a port, offshore installation or structure, pilot station or any other place situated within the inshore traffic zone, or to avoid immediate danger.

(e) A vessel other than a crossing vessel or a vessel joining or leaving a lane shall not normally enter a separation zone or cross a separation line except:

(i) in cases of emergency to avoid immediate danger;

(ii) to engage in fishing within a separation zone.

(f) A vessel navigating in areas near the terminations of traffic separation schemes shall do so with particular caution.

(g) A vessel shall so far as practicable avoid anchoring in a traffic separation scheme or in areas near its terminations.

(h) A vessel not using a traffic separation scheme shall avoid it by as wide a margin as is practicable.

(i) A vessel engaged in fishing shall not impede the passage of any vessel following a traffic lane.

(j) A vessel of less than 20 meters in length or a sailing vessel shall not impede the safe passage of a power-driven vessel following a traffic lane.

(k) A vessel restricted in her ability to maneuver when engaged in an operation for the maintenance of safety of navigation in a traffic separation scheme is exempted from complying with this Rule to the extent necessary to carry out the operation.

(l) A vessel restricted in her ability to maneuver when engaged in an operation for the laying, servicing or picking up of a submarine cable, within a traffic separation scheme, is exempted from complying with this Rule to the extent necessary to carry out the operation.

RULE 10

Traffic Separation Schemes

What It Means

Rule 10 applies only to traffic separation schemes in International Waters that have been formally adopted by the International Maritime Organization (IMO), plus the similar vessel traffic services in U.S. Inland Waters. Such schemes are marked in magenta on charts. The COLREGS apply within a TSS, just as elsewhere. When risk of collision arises within a TSS, all of the COLREGS rules, in addition to Rule 10, apply.

Who must use a TSS? Any vessel proceeding in the general direction of the TSS traffic lanes, except sailboats, motorboats less than twenty meters in length, and boats engaged in fishing, provided there is a separate inshore traffic zone available. Any vessel is permitted to transit an inshore traffic zone, however, to reach a location within it, or in order to avoid immediate danger.

Be especially careful near terminations because boats will be heading out in all directions.

Fishing is allowed both in traffic lanes and in the separation zone between lanes. However:

- Boats fishing in a traffic lane must move in the general direction of traffic and must not impede the passage of any other boat using the lane.
- Boats fishing in a separation zone may proceed in any direction but must not let their nets extend into a traffic zone and impede the passage of any other boat using the traffic lane.

When operating in the vicinity of a traffic separation scheme, find the VHF radio channel used by vessels transiting the scheme and monitor it, particularly in conditions of limited visibility.

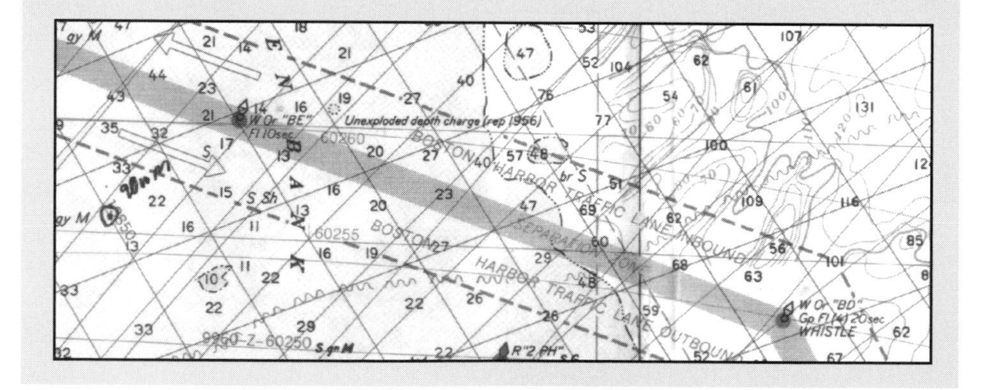

SECTION 2 CONDUCT OF VESSELS IN SIGHT OF ONE ANOTHER

Rule 11: Application

What It Says

Rules in this section apply to vessels in sight of one another.

What It Means

Note that "in sight" means able to be observed by eye; it does not refer to the use of radar.

Rule 12: Sailing Vessels

What It Says

(a) When two sailing vessels are approaching one another, so as to involve risk of collision, one of them shall keep out of the way of the other as follows:

- (i) when each has the wind on a different side, the vessel which has the wind on the port side shall keep out of the way of the other;
- (ii) when both have the wind on the same side, the vessel which is to windward shall keep out of the way of the vessel which is to leeward;
- (iii) if a vessel with the wind on the port side sees a vessel to windward and cannot determine with certainty whether the other vessel has the wind on the port or on the starboard side, she shall keep out of the way of the other.

(b) For the purposes of this Rule the windward side shall be deemed to be the side opposite to that on which the mainsail is carried or, in the case of a square-rigged vessel, the side opposite to that on which the largest fore-and-aft sail is carried.

The italicized text indicates where the Inland Rules differ substantially from the COLREGS.

What It Means

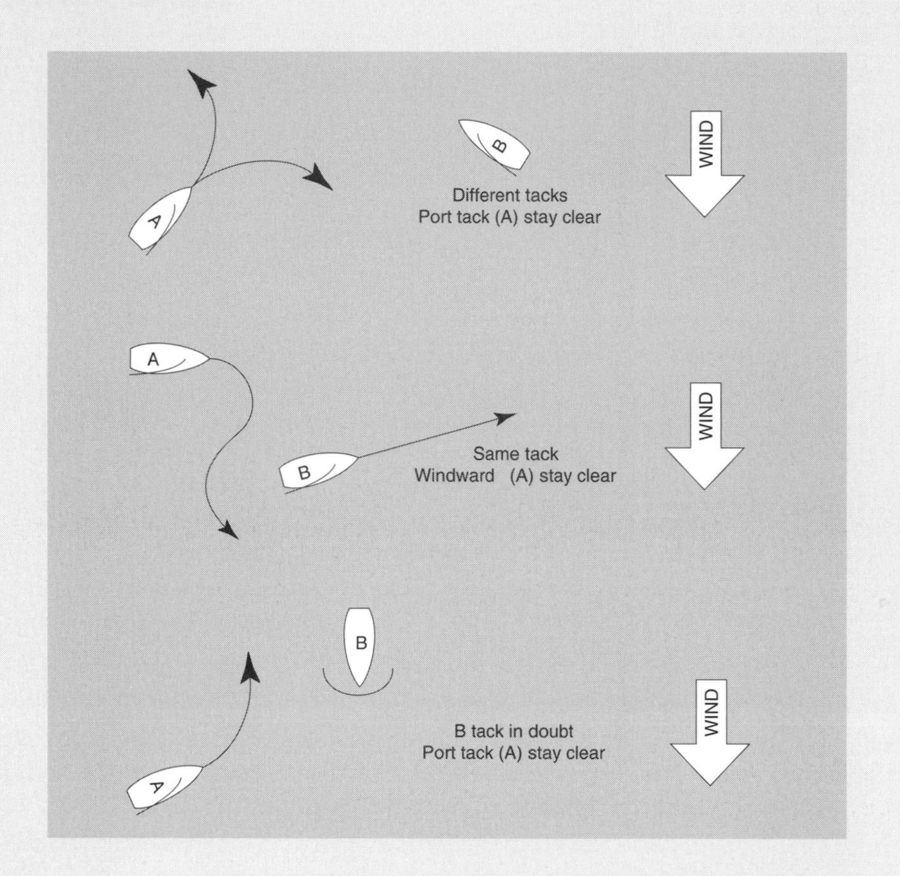

A sailboat is a "sailing vessel" only when she is using her sails as her only source of propulsion. The common practice of motorsailing—using the engine to help the sails— renders a sailboat a "power-driven vessel" for the purposes of the Rules. Be aware that many novice sailboaters aren't aware of this distinction and may assume they are the stand-on vessel in an encounter with a motorboat.

The "tack" of a sailboat is not the side the wind is coming over, but the side opposite that on which the main sail is carried. Of course,

(continued)

the two are the same ninety-nine percent of the time, but the location of the main sail is more easily seen from another boat than is the direction of the wind. Note that in the case of a square-rigged ship, the tack is determined by the largest fore-and-aft sail.

Sailors must remember that Rules 13, 16, 17, and 18 also apply when risk of collision exists between two sailboats:

- Rule 13 (Overtaking) overrules Rule 12 when one of the sailboats is overtaking the other from more than 22.5° abaft the beam.
- Rules 16 (Action by Give-way Vessel) and 17 (Action by Stand-on Vessel) apply to two sailboats, just as to other types of vessels.
- Rule 18 states that a sailboat must keep out of the way of another sailboat that is both sailing and fishing and any other boat that is not under command. Given the definition of fishing in the Rules (does not include angling or sport-trolling), it is unlikely that you will encounter a boat both sailing and fishing anywhere but in a third-world country.

Rule 13: Overtaking

What It Says

(a) Notwithstanding anything contained in the Rules of Part B: Sections I and 2 *(Rules 4–18)*, any vessel overtaking any other shall keep out of the way of the vessel being overtaken.

(b) A vessel shall be deemed to be overtaking when coming up with another vessel from a direction more than 22.5 degrees abaft her beam, that is, in such a position with reference to the vessel she is overtaking, that at night she would be able to see only the sternlight of that vessel but neither of her sidelights.

(c) When a vessel is in any doubt as to whether she is overtaking another, she shall assume that this is the case and act accordingly.

(d) Any subsequent alteration of the bearing between the two vessels shall not make the overtaking vessel a crossing vessel within the meaning of these Rules or relieve her of the duty of keeping clear of the overtaken vessel until she is finally past and clear.

What It Means

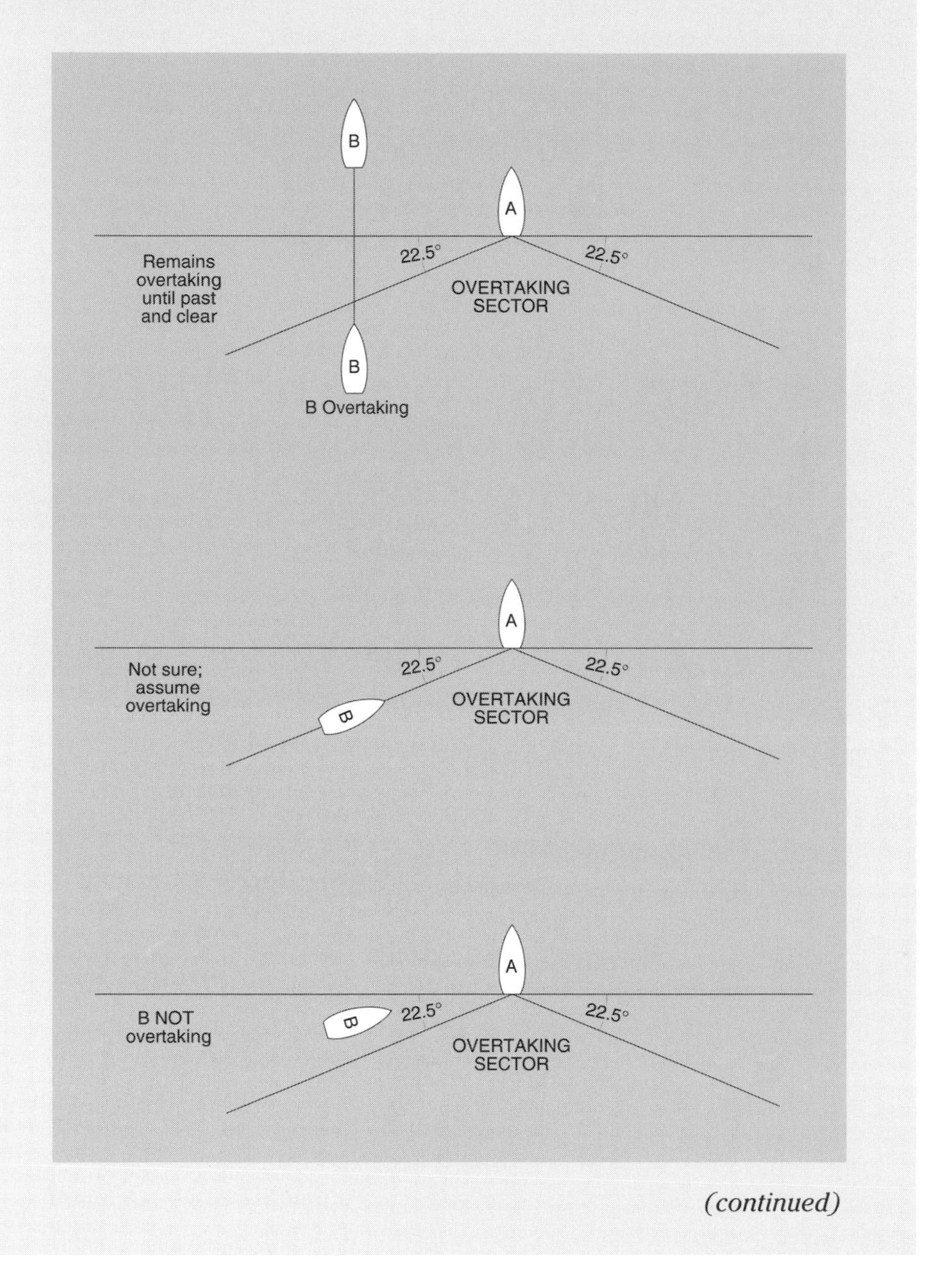

(continued)

Since an overtaken boat is likely to be slower and, thus, less able to get out of the way, an overtaking vessel must always give way.

If the other boat's sidelight is visible at the same time as its sternlight, then the situation is crossing, rather than overtaking.

During daylight, without benefit of the other boat's lights, it may be hard to tell whether you are overtaking, since the 22.5° aft-of-the-beam bearing is defined relative to the beam of the overtaken boat, not that of the overtaking boat. For this reason, Rule 13(c) states that, when there is any doubt, a vessel should assume she is overtaking.

At some time during the overtaking maneuver, the overtaking boat will obviously pull forward of the overtaking sector. For this reason, Rule 13(d) states that an overtaking boat continues to be the give-way boat until she is past and clear of the overtaken boat.

An interesting scenario: Boat 1 passes slower Boat 2, at a great distance, on Boat 2's starboard side. Boat 1 then turns, to cross Boat 2 from Boat 2's starboard side. Does Boat 1 have the right in the new crossing situation, or has she failed to keep out of the way until past and clear?

If such a case went to court, the key issue would probably be whether risk of collision had existed before Boat 1 turned to become a crossing boat. If the passing had taken place at such a distance that risk of collision had never existed, then Boat 1 would never have been an overtaking vessel and, thus, never charged with staying clear. In case of doubt, however, the passing boat would be wise to keep out of the way and not push a questionable claim.

Just because an overtaking boat is burdened with keeping out of the way of an overtaken boat, Rule 13 does not give sailboats, boats of less than twenty meters in length, and fishing boats the right to impede the passage of an overtaking boat in a narrow channel or traffic lane. However, the overtaking boat must first obtain agreement from the overtaken boat and take whatever precautions she can to make the overtaking safe.

Head-On Situation

Rule 14: Head-On Situation

What It Says

(a) *(Unless otherwise agreed)* When two power-driven vessels are meeting on reciprocal or nearly reciprocal courses so as to involve risk of collision each shall alter her course to starboard so that each shall pass on the port side of the other.

(b) Such a situation shall be deemed to exist when a vessel sees the other ahead or nearly ahead and by night she could see the masthead lights of the other in a line or nearly in a line and/or both sidelights and by day she observes the corresponding aspect of the other vessel.

(c) When a vessel is in any doubt as to whether such a situation exists she shall assume that it does exist and act accordingly.

(d) Notwithstanding paragraph (a) of this Rule, a power-driven vessel operating on the Great Lakes, Western Rivers, or waters specified by the Secretary, and proceeding downbound with a following current shall have the right-of-way over an upbound vessel, shall propose the manner of passage, and shall initiate the maneuvering signals prescribed by Rule 34 (a)(1), as appropriate.

What It Means

Note that the rule applies only to powerboats, not to vessels that are sailing, fishing, restricted-in-ability-to-maneuver, or not-under-command.

Note also the phrase "so as to involve risk of collision." Although the rule states that boats meeting head-on should pass port-to-port, this does not mean that you can never pass starboard-to-starboard. Before a risk of collision exists, either boat can alter course so long as the course change requires no subsequent action by the other vessel.

Once risk of collision exists, or when the boats are within a half-mile of each other, U.S. Inland Rules state that the boats must indicate their maneuvers or intent to maneuver with the signals of Rule 34. They may agree to pass starboard-to-starboard, but they should have a good reason to do so.

It is increasingly common under Inland Rules for boats to signal their intentions via VHF radio, referring to port-to-port as "one whistle" and starboard-to-starboard as "two whistles." This may be acceptable

(continued)

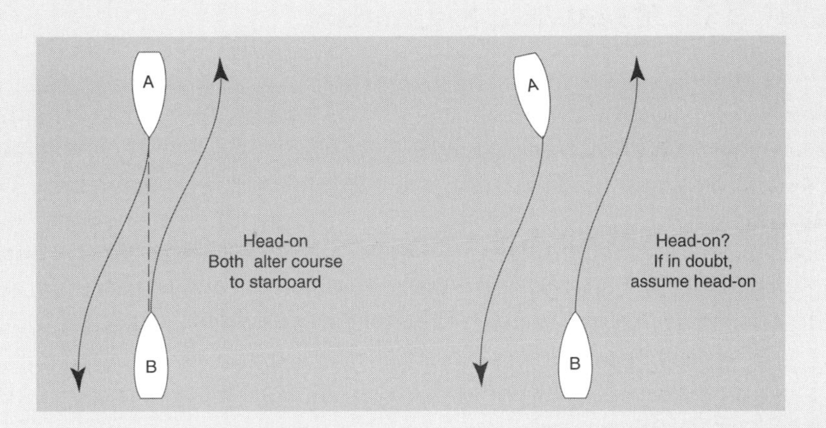

between professional mariners but is very dangerous between weekend boaters, since some skippers don't understand the meanings and may be reluctant to admit it in front of their passengers. In the interest of safety, pass port-to-port whenever possible and indicate your intentions in those words.

A "reciprocal or nearly reciprocal course" is:

- when a boat sees another boat ahead or nearly ahead;
- when at night she sees the masthead lights of the other in a line or nearly in a line;
- when at night she sees both sidelights.

Of the three criteria, the third is the most precise because sidelights are designed to shine only one–three degrees to the opposite side of the centerline, so that when both lights are seen simultaneously, the two boats are theoretically within about two degrees of head-on. Allowing for yawing, if you see both sidelights simultaneously, either constantly or occasionally, then the boat is within about five degrees of head-on.

A fine distinction, which could become important in a strong cross current, is whether the rule truly means reciprocal courses (referring to the direction of motion) or reciprocal headings (referring to the direction in which the boat is pointed). Paragraph 14(a) indicates course, but paragraph 14(b) says that a reciprocal course shall be deemed to exist when both sidelights can be seen, indicating a reciprocal heading. Paragraph 14(c) resolves the conflict by stating that, in case of doubt, you are to assume that the situation is head-on.

RULE

15

Crossing Situation

Rule 15: Crossing Situation

What It Says

(a) When two power-driven vessels are crossing so as to involve risk of collision, the vessel which has the other on her own starboard side shall keep out of the way and shall, if the circumstances of the case admit, avoid crossing ahead of the other vessel.

(b) Notwithstanding paragraph (a), on the Great Lakes, Western Rivers, or water specified by the Secretary, a vessel crossing a river shall keep out of the way of a power-driven vessel ascending or descending the river.

What It Means

Note that Rule 15 applies only:

- to two boats, not three or more;
- to power-driven boats (not to boats that are sailing, fishing, not under command, or restricted in their ability to maneuver);
- in crossing (not head-on or overtaking) situations;
- after risk of collision has been determined to exist.

Before risk of collision has been established, either boat is free to maneuver at will. Once risk of collision has been established, however, the boat with the other vessel approaching on her starboard side:

- becomes the give-way boat;
- must not cross ahead of the stand-on boat unless circumstances require it.

Remember that a boat approaching on your starboard side sees your green (go) light, while a boat approaching on your port side sees your red (stop) light.

Before crossing a narrow channel, remember Rule 9(d), "A vessel shall not cross a narrow channel or fairway if such crossing impedes the passage of a vessel which can safely navigate only within such channel or fairway."

Similarly, when you are in a traffic separation scheme, remember that Rule 10(j) states, "A vessel of less than 20 meters in length ... shall not impede the safe passage of a power-driven vessel following a traffic lane."

(continued)

When an ordinary power-driven boat meets a fishing or hampered boat, Rule 18, rather than Rule 15, applies. Therefore, if your power boat is approached on its port side by a fishing or hampered boat, you must keep clear. You are not, however, forbidden to cross ahead of the stand-on boat, as you would be under Rule 15.

The rules governing a situation in which a power boat meets a boat constrained by her draft contain subtle distinctions. First, the boat constrained by her draft can only claim those special rights by displaying the proper signals. Provided the signals are displayed, then the ordinary power boat must "avoid impeding the safe passage of the vessel constrained by her draft" by taking action before risk of collision develops. However, once risk of collision has been established, a constrained-by-draft boat approaching on the port side of an ordinary power boat becomes the give-way boat under Rule 15.

A power boat underway, but not making way through the water, has no special rights. If she is stopped because she is either anchored or broken down (not under command), then she should display the proper anchored or not-under-command signals. If not, and if she is approached by another power boat from dead ahead to 22.5 degrees abaft her starboard beam, then she'd better get some way on and get out of the way!

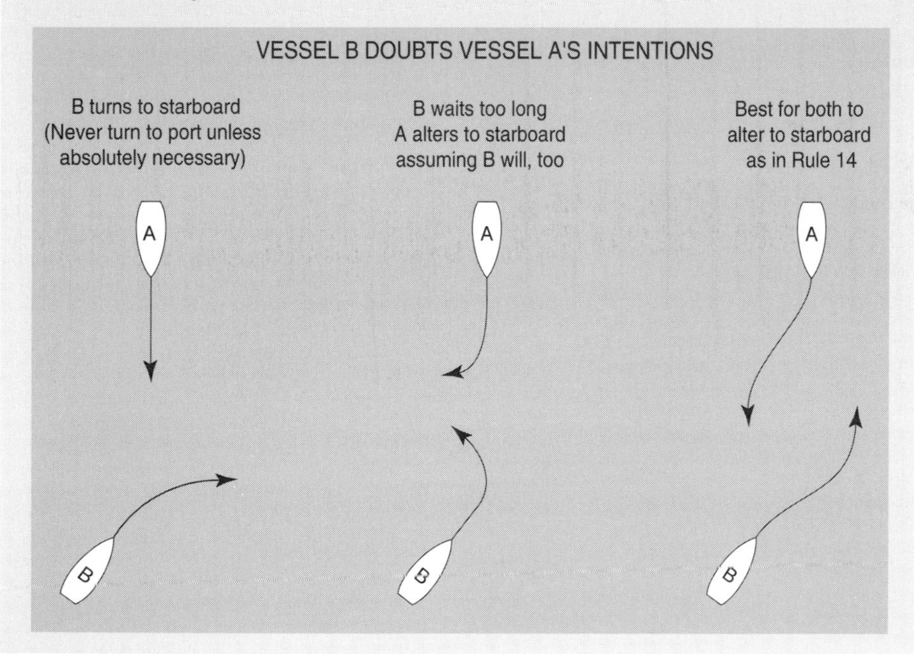

Rule 16: Action by Give-Way Vessel

What It Says

Every vessel that is directed to keep out of the way of another vessel shall, so far as possible, take early and substantial action to keep well clear.

What It Means

In essence, Rule 16 simply states that a give-way vessel must give way in the manner prescribed in Rule 8.

Rule 17: Action by Stand-On Vessel

What It Says

(a) (i) Where one of two vessels is to keep out of the way, the other shall keep her course and speed.
(ii) The latter vessel may, however, take action to avoid collision by her maneuver alone, as soon as it becomes apparent to her that the vessel required to keep out of the way is not taking appropriate action in compliance with these Rules.

(b) When, from any cause, the vessel required to keep her course and speed finds herself so close that collision cannot be avoided by the action of the give-way vessel alone, she shall take such action as will best aid to avoid collision.

(c) A power-driven vessel which takes action in a crossing situation in accordance with subparagraph (a)(ii) of this Rule to avoid collision with another power-driven vessel shall, if the circumstances of the case admit, not alter course to port for a vessel on her own port side.

(d) This Rule does not relieve the give-way vessel of her obligation to keep out of the way.

What It Means

Rule 17 applies only where risk of collision exists between two (not three or more) boats. In such a situation, the boat required to keep out of the way is the "give-way vessel" (Rule 16). Rule 17 covers the other boat, the "stand-on vessel."

The actions permitted/required of the stand-on vessel take place in four stages:

1. Before risk of collision exists, either boat is free to maneuver at will.
2. Once risk of collision exists, except to avoid hazards, the stand-on boat must maintain course and speed.
3. If it becomes apparent to the stand-on boat that the give-way boat is not taking the appropriate (early and substantial) action to keep out of the way, then the stand-on boat is *permitted* to take action to avoid collision. If both boats are power-driven, however, the action must not be a turn to port for a give-way boat on her port. Any maneuver she makes must be accompanied by the appropriate maneuvering signal in Rule 34. If she chooses not to maneuver, then she should sound the danger signal (five short whistles) as a wake-up call to the unresponsive give-way boat. If the give-way vessel is readily identified either by name, characteristics, or location, then a call on VHF CH13 or 16 would be appropriate, in addition.

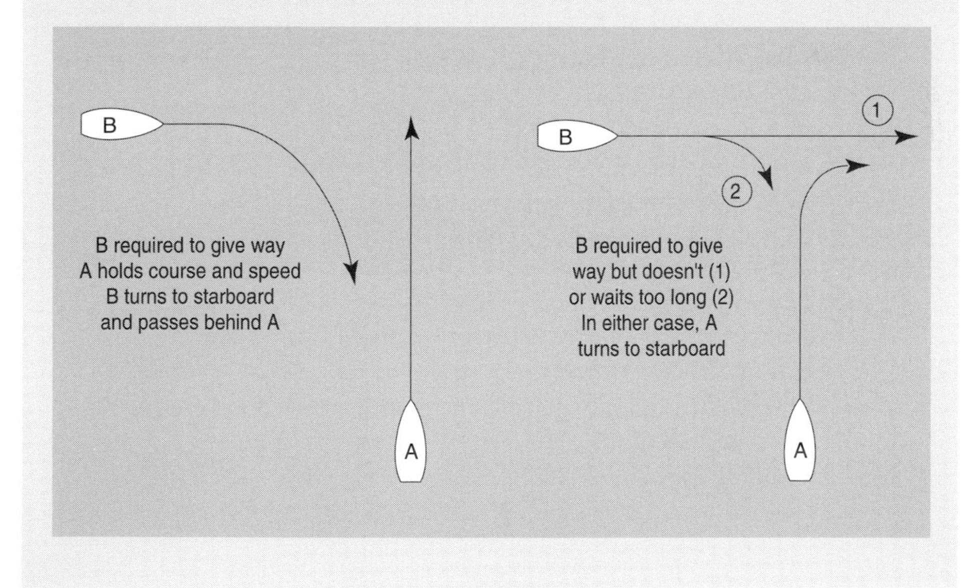

4. If the situation deteriorates to the point where collision can no longer be avoided by action of the give-way boat alone, the stand-on boat is *required* to take the best action it can to avoid collision. Again, the action should be accompanied by the appropriate sound signals. At this late stage, a turn to port is not absolutely prohibited. In fact, if it appears that the give-way boat is about to strike the stand-on boat aft, a hard turn to port might be the best maneuver to avoid collision.

The timing and nature of a stand-on boat's Stage 3 actions are critical. If she takes action too soon, she may find herself acting simultaneously with the give-way boat. To prevent escalation of the confusion, the stand-on boat should always:

- turn to starboard;
- accompany the maneuver with the appropriate signal so that the give-way boat understands her action.

Rule 18: Responsibilities Between Vessels

What It Says

Except where Rules 9, 10, and 13 otherwise require:

(a) A power-driven vessel underway shall keep out of the way of:
(i) a vessel not under command;
(ii) a vessel restricted in her ability to maneuver;
(iii) a vessel engaged in fishing; and
(iv) a sailing vessel.

(b) A sailing vessel underway shall keep out of the way of:
(i) a vessel not under command;
(ii) a vessel restricted in her ability to maneuver; and
(iii) a vessel engaged in fishing.

(c) A vessel engaged in fishing when underway shall, so far as possible, keep out of the way of:
(i) a vessel not under command;
(ii) a vessel restricted in her ability to maneuver.

(d) (i) A vessel other than a vessel not under command or a vessel restricted in her ability to maneuver shall, if the circumstances of the case admit, avoid impeding the safe passage of a vessel constrained by her draft, exhibiting the signals in Rule 28.
(ii) A vessel constrained by her draft shall navigate with particular caution having full regard to her special condition.

Note that there is no mention of a "vessel constrained by her draft" anywhere in the Inland Rules.

(e) A seaplane on the water shall, in general, keep well clear of all vessels and avoid impeding their navigation. In circumstances, however, where risk of collision exists, she shall comply with the Rules of this Part.

What It Means

Rule 18 applies to all situations except for:

- Narrow channels (Rule 9)
- Traffic separation schemes (Rule 10)
- Overtaking situations (Rule 13)

The rule establishes a "pecking order" between types of boats. Boats higher than you on the list are considered the "stand-on" vessel in a collision situation; vessels below you are the "give-way" vessel. The top two (vessel not under command and vessel restricted in ability to maneuver) share equal status, however. The list, in order of decreasing rights:

- Vessel not under command, and vessel restricted in ability to maneuver
- Vessel constrained by draft
- Vessel engaged in fishing
- Sailing vessel
- Power-driven vessel
- Seaplane

Example: A sailboat (powered by sail alone) must keep out of the way of vessels engaged in fishing, constrained by draft, restricted in ability to maneuver, and not under command (all of the vessel types above it in the list), but not ordinary power boats or seaplanes.

To claim special status, a boat must display the appropriate lights or shapes. Therefore, a fishing boat not displaying fishing or trawling lights or shapes and a tug not displaying the lights or shapes for a vessel restricted in ability to maneuver are to be considered simply power-driven vessels. A sailboat while motorsailing, however, reverses this logic. By displaying a cone, apex down (required of all motorsailing vessels except those less than twelve meters under Inland Rules), it drops in status from sailing to power-driven.

(continued)

Since the special privilege signals are often not spotted or identified (probably less than ten percent of all recreational boaters would be able to identify such signals), privileged boats should always be prepared to sound the danger signal (five short blasts).

SECTION 3 CONDUCT OF VESSELS IN RESTRICTED VISIBILITY

Rule 19: Conduct of Vessels in Restricted Visibility

What It Says

The italicized text indicates where the Inland Rules differ substantially from the COLREGS.

(a) This Rule applies to vessels not in sight of one another when navigating in or near an area of restricted visibility.

(b) Every vessel shall proceed at a safe speed adapted to the prevailing circumstances and conditions of restricted visibility. A power-driven vessel shall have her engines ready for immediate maneuver.

(c) Every vessel shall have due regard to the prevailing circumstances and conditions of restricted visibility when complying with Rules of Section I of this Part *(Rules 4 through 10)*.

(d) A vessel which detects by radar alone the presence of another vessel shall determine if a close-quarters situation is developing and/or risk of collision exists. If so, she shall take avoiding action in ample time, provided that when such action consists of an alteration of course, so far as possible the following shall be avoided:

(i) an alteration of course to port for a vessel forward of the beam, other than for a vessel being overtaken; and

(ii) an alteration of course toward a vessel abeam or abaft the beam.

(e) Except where it has been determined that a risk of collision does not exist, every vessel which hears apparently forward of her beam the fog signal of another vessel, or which cannot avoid a close-quarters situation with another vessel forward of her beam, shall reduce her speed to the minimum at which she can be kept on course. She shall if necessary take all her way off and, in any event, navigate with extreme caution until danger of collision is over.

RULE

19

Conduct of Vessels in Restricted Visibility

What It Means

Rule 19 applies only to boats, in or near restricted visibility, that can not see each other by eye. If the boats subsequently do see each other, Rules 11–18 take over.

The phrase "in or near an area of restricted visibility" is more important than one might think. Courts have found that a boat failing to slow to safe speed before entering an area of restricted visibility is just as liable as one speeding inside the area. The point is that a boat outside the area cannot see a boat inside the area and vice-versa. The visibility is no greater than if both were inside the area.

Rule 19 repeats the injunction of Rule 6 to, at all times, proceed at a safe speed. This is a very hard rule to follow in fog, as the courts have repeatedly judged "safe speed" to be that which would allow stopping in one-half the distance of visibility. For any vessel in dense fog, this translates into stopping altogether!

Rule 19(b) also instructs a power boat to keep her "engines ready for immediate maneuver." She would, however, probably be excused for shutting her engines down briefly in order to better listen for sound signals. "Ready for immediate maneuver" presumably includes the steering mechanism. If so, a boat in limited visibility should be on manual steering—not autopilot—and the helmsman should have one hand on the throttle.

The phrase, "so far as possible," is inserted in paragraph 19(d) to allow for the possibility of limited sea room due to navigational hazards or the near presence of other boats.

Paragraph 19(e) refers to "except where it has been determined that a risk of collision does not exist." The only defensible, yet still risky, method of making such a determination in fog is through a series of radar bearings. If you don't have radar, or are not proficient in taking and plotting radar bearings, you obviously cannot say that you have determined there to be no risk.

Unless you have determined there is no risk of collision, when you hear a fog signal forward of your beam or otherwise find yourself in close quarters with another boat forward of your beam, you must reduce your speed to bare steerageway, or even stop dead in the water. Also, while Rule 35 specifies the maximum interval between fog signals, it does not prevent blowing your horn more often.

(continued)

Finally, not mentioned in the Rules, but prudent behavior: If you hear a boat approaching from forward of your beam, you might want to take all way off. First, however, turn to face the other boat head-on, for two reasons:

- To present a smaller target.
- To take a possible blow at your boat's least vulnerable point—her bow.

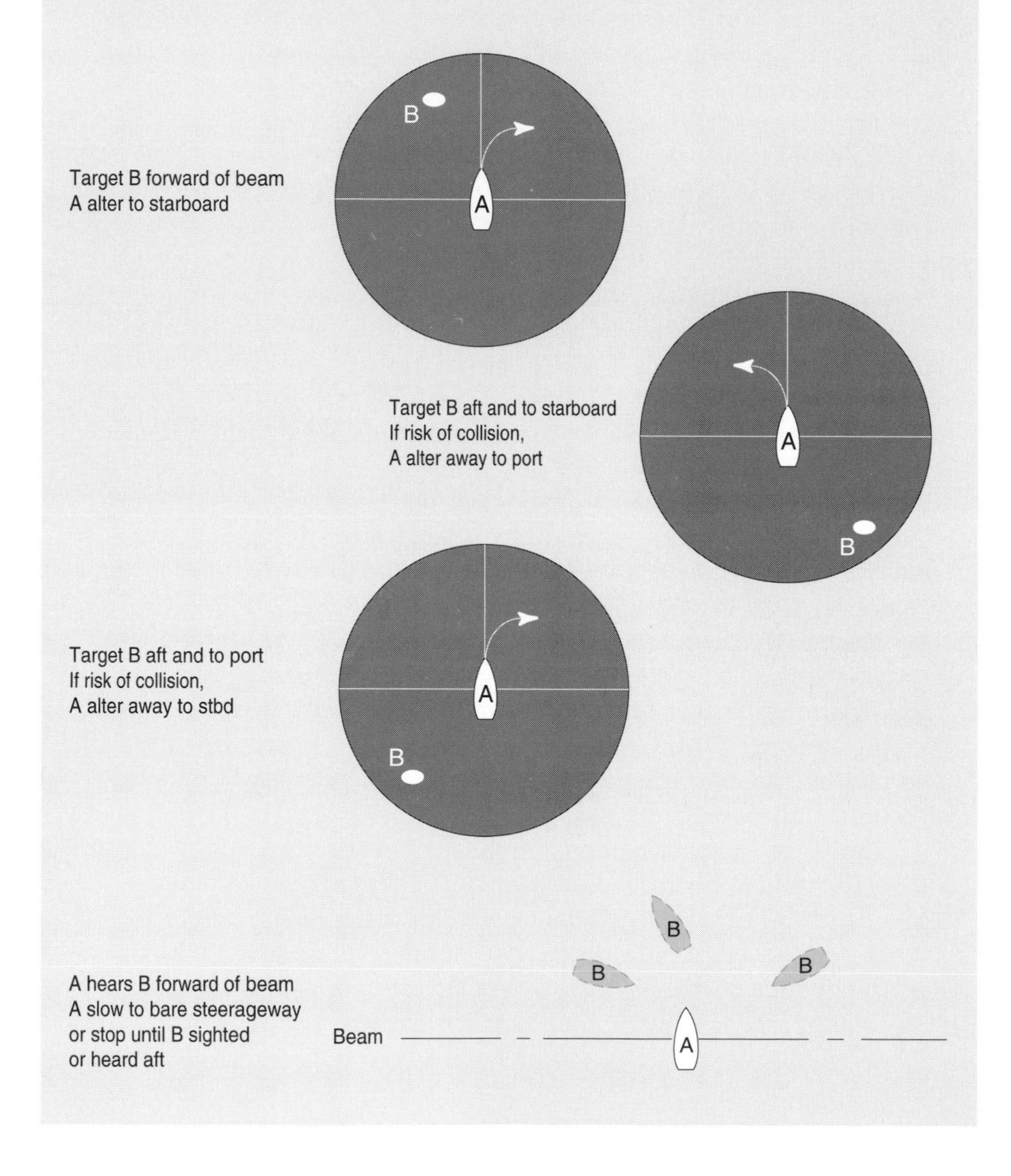

PART C: Lights and Shapes

RULE

20

Application

Rule 20: Application

What It Says

(a) Rules in this Part shall be complied with in all weathers.
(b) The Rules concerning lights shall be complied with from sunset to sunrise, and during such times no other lights shall be exhibited, except such lights as cannot be mistaken for the lights specified in these Rules or do not impair their visibility or distinctive character, or interfere with the keeping of a proper lookout.
(c) The lights prescribed by these Rules shall, if carried, also be exhibited from sunrise to sunset in restricted visibility and may be exhibited in all other circumstances when it is deemed necessary.
(d) The Rules concerning shapes shall be complied with by day.
(e) The lights and shapes specified in these Rules shall comply with the provisions of Annex I of these Regulations.

The italicized text indicates where the Inland Rules differ substantially from the COLREGS.

What It Means

Lights must be displayed at night (sunset to sunrise) and during the day in restricted visibility. Shapes must be displayed from sunrise to sunset, regardless of visibility. Lights that could be confused with the official lights or affect the lookout are prohibited.

RULE

21

Definitions

Rule 21: Definitions

What It Says

(a) "Masthead light" means a white light placed over the fore and aft centerline of the vessel showing an unbroken light over an arc of the horizon of 225 degrees and so fixed as to show the light from right ahead to 22.5 degrees abaft the beam on either side of the vessel *(except that on a vessel of less than 12 meters in length the masthead light shall be placed as nearly as practicable to the fore and aft centerline of the vessel).*

(b) "Sidelights" mean a green light on the starboard side and a red light on the port side each showing an unbroken light over an arc of the horizon of 112.5 degrees and so fixed as to show the light from right ahead to 22.5 degrees abaft the beam on its respective side. In a vessel of less than 20 meters in length the sidelights may be combined in one lantern carried on the fore and aft centerline of the vessel *(except that on a vessel of less than 12 meters in length the sidelights when combined in one lantern shall be placed as nearly as practicable to the fore and aft centerline of the vessel).*

(c) "Sternlight" means a white light placed as nearly as practicable at the stern showing an unbroken light over an arc of the horizon of 135 degrees and so fixed as to show the light 67.5 degrees from right aft on each side of the vessel.

(d) "Towing light" means a yellow light having the same characteristics as the "sternlight" defined in paragraph (c) of this Rule.

(e) "All-round light" means a light showing an unbroken light over an arc of the horizon of 360 degrees.

(f) "Flashing light" means a light flashing at regular intervals at a frequency of 120 flashes or more per minute.

(g) "Special flashing light"means a yellow light flashing at regular intervals at a frequency of 50 to 70 flashes per minute, placed as far forward and as nearly as practicable on the fore and aft centerline of the tow and showing an unbroken light over an arc of the horizon of not less than 180 degrees nor more than 225 degrees and so fixed as to show the light from right ahead to abeam and no more than 22.5 degrees abaft the beam on either side of the vessel.

What It Means

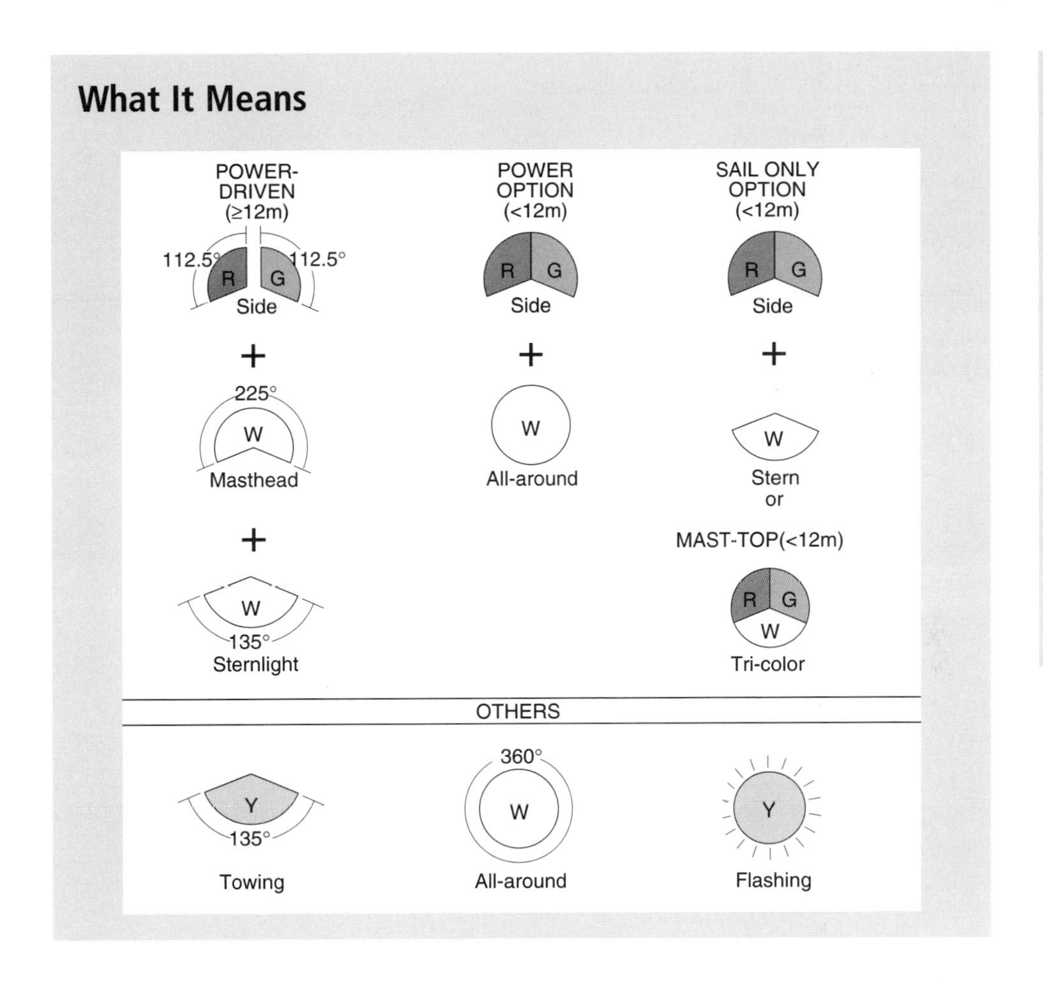

Rule 22: Visibility of Lights

What It Says

The lights prescribed in these Rules shall have an intensity as specified in Section 8 of Annex I to these Rules, so as to be visible at the following minimum ranges:

(a) In a vessel of 50 meters or more in length:

—a masthead light, 6 miles;

—a sidelight, 3 miles;

—a sternlight, 3 miles;

—a towing light, 3 miles;

—a white, red, green or yellow all-round light, 3 miles; and

—a special flashing light, 2 miles.

(b) In a vessel of 12 meters or more in length but less than 50 meters in length:
—a masthead light, 5 miles; except that where the length of the vessel is less than 20 meters, 3 miles;
—a sidelight, 2 miles;
—a sternlight, 2 miles;
—a towing light, 2 miles;
—a white, red, green or yellow all-round light, 2 miles; and
—a special flashing light, 2 miles.

(c) In a vessel of less than 12 meters in length:
—a masthead light, 2 miles;
—a sidelight, 1 mile;
—a sternlight, 2 miles;
—a towing light, 2 miles;
—a white, red, green or yellow all-round light, 2 miles; and
—a special flashing light, 2 miles.

(d) In an inconspicuous, partly submerged vessel or object being towed:
—a white all-round light, 3 miles.

What It Means

Type of light*	Vessel length in meters	Visibility in miles
MASTHEAD	under 12	2
	12–20	3
	20–50	5
	over 50	6
SIDE	under 12	1
	12–50	2
	over 50	3
STERN, TOWING, AND ALL-AROUND	under 50	2
	over 50	3

* Note also that inconspicuous, partly submerged vessels or objects being towed should carry a white all-around light, visible at a distance of three miles. *The Inland Rules also specify, for vessels of all lengths, a special flashing light, visible at a distance of two miles.*

Rule 23: Power-Driven Vessels Underway

What It Says

(a) A power-driven vessel underway shall exhibit:

(i) a masthead light forward; *except that a vessel of less than 20 meters in length need not exhibit this light forward of amidships but shall exhibit it as far forward as is practicable;*

(ii) a second masthead light abaft of and higher than the forward one; except that a vessel of less than 50 meters in length shall not be obliged to exhibit such light but may do so;

(iii) sidelights;

(iv) a stern light.

(b) An air-cushion vessel when operating in the nondisplacement mode shall, in addition to the lights prescribed in paragraph (a) of this Rule, exhibit an all-round flashing yellow light *(where it can best be seen).*

(c) (i) A power-driven vessel of less than 12 meters in length may in lieu of the lights prescribed in paragraph (a) of this Rule exhibit an all-round white light and sidelights;

(ii) a power-driven vessel of less than 7 meters in length whose maximum speed does not exceed 7 knots may in lieu of the lights prescribed in paragraph (a) of this Rule exhibit an all round white light and shall, if practicable, also exhibit sidelights;

(iii) the masthead light or all-round white light on a power-driven vessel of less than 12 meters in length may be displaced from the fore and aft centerline of the vessel if centerline fitting is not practicable, provided that the sidelights are combined in one lantern which shall be carried on the fore and aft centerline of the vessel or located as nearly as practicable in the same fore and aft line as the masthead light or the all-round white light.

(d) A power-driven vessel when operating on the Great Lakes may carry an all-round white light in lieu of the second masthead light and sternlight prescribed in paragraph (a) of this Rule. The light shall be carried in the position of the second masthead light and be visible at the same minimum range.

What It Means (Rule 23)

See illustration on page 34.

Rule 24: Towing and Pushing

What It Says

(a) A power-driven vessel when towing shall exhibit:

(i) instead of the light prescribed in Rule 23(a)(i) or (a)(ii), two masthead lights in a vertical line. When the length of the tow, measuring from the stern of the towing vessel to the after end of the tow exceeds 200 meters, three such lights in a vertical line;

(ii) sidelights;

(iii) a sternlight;

(iv) a towing light in a vertical line above the sternlight;

(v) when the length of the tow exceeds 200 meters, a diamond shape where it can best be seen.

(b) When a pushing vessel and a vessel being pushed ahead are rigidly connected in a composite unit they shall be regarded as a power-driven vessel and exhibit the lights prescribed in Rule 23.

(c) A power-driven vessel when pushing ahead or towing alongside, except in the case of a composite unit *(except as required by paragraphs (b) and (i) of this Rule)*, shall exhibit:

(i) instead of the light prescribed in Rule 23(a)(i) or (a)(ii), two masthead lights in a vertical line;

(ii) sidelights;

(iii) a stern light *(two towing lights in a vertical line)*.

(d) A power-driven vessel to which paragraph (a) or (c) of this Rule apply shall also comply with Rule 23(a)(ii) *(and Rule 23(a)(i))*.

(e) A vessel or object being towed, other than those mentioned in paragraph (g) of this Rule, shall exhibit:

(i) sidelights;

(ii) a sternlight;

(iii) when the length of the tow exceeds 200 meters, a diamond shape where it can best be seen.

(f) Provided that any number of vessels being towed alongside or pushed in a group shall be lighted as one vessel,

(i) a vessel being pushed ahead, not being part of a composite unit,

shall exhibit at the forward end, sidelights *(and a special flashing light)*;
(ii) a vessel being towed alongside shall exhibit a sternlight and at the forward end, sidelights.

(g) An inconspicuous, partly submerged vessel or object, or combination of such vessels or objects being towed, shall exhibit:

(i) if it is less than 25 meters in breadth, one all-round white light at or near the forward end and one at or near the after end except that dracones need not exhibit a light at or near the forward end;

(ii) if it is 25 meters or more in breadth, two additional all-round white lights at or near the extremities of its breadth *(four all-round white lights to mark its length and breadth)*;

(iii) if it exceeds 100 meters in length, additional all-round white lights between the lights prescribed in subparagraphs (i) and (ii) so that the distance between the lights shall not exceed 100 meters *(Provided, that any vessels or objects being towed alongside each other shall be lighted as one vessel or object)*;

(iv) a diamond shape at or near the aftermost extremity of the last vessel or object being towed and if the length of the tow exceeds 200 meters an additional diamond shape where it can best be seen and located as far forward as is practicable.

(v) the towing vessel may direct a searchlight in the direction of the tow to indicate its presence to an approaching vessel.

(h) Where from any sufficient cause it is impracticable for a vessel or object being towed to exhibit the lights or shapes prescribed in paragraph (e) or (g) of this Rule, all possible measures shall be taken to light the vessel or object towed or at least to indicate the presence of such vessel or object.

(i) Notwithstanding paragraph (c), on the Western Rivers (except below the Huey P. Long Bridge on the Mississippi River) and on waters specified by the Secretary, a power-driven vessel when pushing ahead or towing alongside, except as paragraph (b) applies, shall exhibit:

(i) sidelights; and

(ii) two towing lights in a vertical line.

(i) *(j)* Where from any sufficient cause it is impracticable for a vessel not normally engaged in towing operations to display the lights prescribed in paragraph (a) or (c) of this Rule, such vessel shall not be required to exhibit those lights when engaged in towing another vessel in distress or otherwise in need of assistance. All possible measures shall be taken to indicate the nature of the relationship between the towing vessel and the vessel being towed as authorized by Rule 36, in particular by illuminating the towline.

What It Means (Rule 24)

See illustration on page 35.

Rule 25: Sailing Vessels Underway and Vessels Under Oars

What It Says

(a) A sailing vessel underway shall exhibit:
(i) sidelights;
(ii) a stern light.

(b) In a sailing vessel of less than 20 meters in length the lights prescribed in paragraph (a) of this Rule may be combined in one lantern carried at or near the top of the mast where it can best be seen.

(c) A sailing vessel underway may, in addition to the lights prescribed in paragraph (a) of this Rule, exhibit at or near the top of the mast, where they can best be seen, two all-round lights in a vertical line, the upper being red and the lower green, but these lights shall not be exhibited in conjunction with the combined lantern permitted by paragraph (b) of this Rule.

(d) (i) A sailing vessel of less than 7 meters in length shall, if practicable, exhibit the lights prescribed in paragraph (a) or (b) of this Rule, but if she does not, she shall have ready at hand an electric torch or lighted lantern showing a white light which shall be exhibited in sufficient time to prevent collision.
(ii) A vessel under oars may exhibit the lights prescribed in this Rule for sailing vessels, but if she does not, she shall have ready at hand an electric torch or lighted lantern showing a white light which shall be exhibited in sufficient time to prevent collision.

(e) A vessel proceeding under sail when also being propelled by machinery shall exhibit forward where it can best be seen a conical shape, apex downwards. *(A vessel of less than 12 meters in length is not required to exhibit this shape, but may do so.)*

What It Means

See illustration on page 36.

RULE

26

Fishing Vessels

Rule 26: Fishing Vessels

What It Says

(a) A vessel engaged in fishing, whether underway or at anchor, shall exhibit only the lights and shapes prescribed in this Rule.
(b) A vessel when engaged in trawling, by which is meant the dragging through the water of a dredge net or other apparatus used as a fishing appliance, shall exhibit:

(i) two all-round lights in a vertical line, the upper being green and the lower white, or a shape consisting of two cones with their apexes together in a vertical line one above the other; *(a vessel of less than 20 meters in length may instead of this shape exhibit a basket);*
(ii) a masthead light abaft of and higher than the all-round green light; a vessel of less than 50 meters in length shall not be obliged to exhibit such a light but may do so;
(iii) when making way through the water, in addition to the lights prescribed in this paragraph, sidelights and a sternlight.

(c) A vessel engaged in fishing, other than trawling, shall exhibit:

(i) two all-round lights in a vertical line, the upper being red and the lower white, or a shape consisting of two cones with apexes together in a vertical line one above the other; *(a vessel of less than 20 meters in length may instead of this shape exhibit a basket);*
(ii) when there is outlying gear extending more than 150 meters horizontally from the vessel, an all-round white light or a cone apex upward in the direction of the gear; and (iii) when making way through the water, in addition to the lights prescribed in this paragraph, sidelights and a sternlight.

(d) The additional signals described in Annex II to these regulations apply to a vessel engaged in fishing in close proximity to other vessels engaged in fishing.
(e) A vessel when not engaged in fishing shall not exhibit the lights or shapes prescribed in this Rule, but only those prescribed for a vessel of her length.

What It Means

See illustration on page 37.

Rule 27: Vessels Not Under Command or Restricted in Their Ability to Maneuver

What It Says

(a) A vessel not under command shall exhibit:

(i) two all-round red lights in a vertical line where they can best be seen;

(ii) two balls or similar shapes in a vertical line where they can best be seen;

(iii) when making way through the water, in addition to the lights prescribed in this paragraph, sidelights and a sternlight.

(b) A vessel restricted in her ability to maneuver, except a vessel engaged in mine-clearance operations, shall exhibit:

(i) three all-round lights in a vertical line where they can best be seen. The highest and lowest of these lights shall be red and the middle light shall be white;

(ii) three shapes in a vertical line where they can best be seen. The highest and lowest of these shapes shall be balls and the middle one a diamond;

(iii) when making way through the water, a masthead light or lights, sidelights and a sternlight, in addition to the lights prescribed in subparagraph *(b)* (i);

(iv) when at anchor, in addition to the lights or shapes prescribed in subparagraphs *(b)* (i) and (ii), the light, lights or shape prescribed in Rule 30.

(c) A power-driven vessel engaged in a towing operation such as severely restricts the towing vessel and her tow in their ability to deviate from their course shall, in addition to the lights or shapes prescribed in Rule 24(a), exhibit the lights or shapes prescribed in sub-paragraphs (b)(i) and (ii) of this Rule,

(d) A vessel engaged in dredging or underwater operations, when restricted in her ability to maneuver, shall exhibit the lights and shapes prescribed in subparagraphs (b)(i), (ii) and (iii) of this Rule and shall in addition, when an obstruction exists, exhibit:

(i) two all-round red lights or two balls in a vertical line to indicate the side on which the obstruction exists;

(ii) two all-round green lights or two diamonds in a vertical line to indicate the side on which another vessel may pass;

(iii) when at anchor, the lights or shapes prescribed in this paragraph instead of the lights or shape prescribed in Rule 30 *(for anchored vessels)*.

(e) Whenever the size of a vessel engaged in diving operations makes it impracticable to exhibit all lights and shapes prescribed in paragraph (d) of this Rule, the following shall be exhibited:

(i) three all-round lights in a vertical line where they can best be seen. The highest and lowest of these lights shall be red and the middle light shall be white;

(ii) a rigid replica of the International Code flag "A" not less than 1 meter in height. Measures shall be taken to ensure its all round visibility.

(f) A vessel engaged in mineclearance operations shall in addition to the lights prescribed for a power-driven vessel in Rule 23 or to the lights or shape prescribed for a vessel at anchor in Rule 30 as appropriate, exhibit three all-round green lights or three balls. One of these lights or shapes shall be exhibited near the foremast head and one at each end of the fore yard. These lights or shapes indicate that it is dangerous for another vessel to approach within 1000 meters of the mine-clearance vessel.

(g) Vessels of less than 12 meters in length, except those engaged in diving operations, shall not be required to exhibit the lights and shapes prescribed in this Rule.

(h) The signals prescribed in this Rule are not signals of vessels in distress and requiring assistance. Such signals are contained in Annex IV to these Regulations.

What It Means

See illustration on page 38.

Rule 28: Vessels Constrained by Their Draft

What It Says

A vessel constrained by her draft may, in addition to the lights prescribed for power-driven vessels in Rule 23, exhibit where they can best be seen three all-round red lights in a vertical line, or a cylinder. *Note: There is no mention of a "vessel constrained by her draft" in the Inland Rules.*

What It Means

See illustration on page 39.

Rule 29: Pilot Vessels

What It Says

(a) A vessel engaged on pilotage duty shall exhibit:

(i) at or near the masthead, two all-round lights in a vertical line, the upper being white and the lower red;

(ii) when underway, in addition, sidelights and a sternlight;

(iii) when at anchor, in addition to the lights prescribed in subparagraph (i), the light, lights or shape prescribed in Rule 30 for vessels at anchor.

(b) A pilot vessel when not engaged on pilotage duty shall exhibit the lights or shapes prescribed for a similar vessel of her length.

What It Means

See illustration on page 39.

Rule 30: Anchored Vessels and Vessels Aground

What It Says

(a) A vessel at anchor shall exhibit where it can best be seen:

(i) in the fore part, an all-round white light or one ball;

(ii) at or near the stern and at a lower level than the light prescribed in subparagraph (i), an all-round white light.

(b) A vessel of less than 50 meters in length may exhibit an all-round white light where it can best be seen instead of the lights prescribed in paragraph (a) of this Rule.

(c) A vessel at anchor may, and a vessel of 100 meters and more in length shall, also use the available working or equivalent lights to illuminate her decks.

(d) A vessel aground shall exhibit the lights prescribed in paragraph (a) or (b) of this Rule and in addition, *(if practicable)* where they can best be seen:

(i) two all-round red lights in a vertical line;

(ii) three balls in a vertical line.

(e) A vessel of less than 7 meters in length, when at anchor, not in or near a narrow channel, fairway or anchorage, or where other vessels normally navigate, shall not be required to exhibit the lights or shape prescribed in paragraphs (a) and (b) of this Rule.

(f) A vessel of less than 12 meters in length, when aground, shall not be required to exhibit the lights or shapes prescribed in subparagraphs (d)(i) and (ii) of this Rule.

(g) A vessel of less than 20 meters in length, when at anchor in a special anchorage area designated by the Secretary, shall not be required to exhibit the anchor lights and shapes required by this Rule.

What It Means

See illustration on page 40.

RULES

31 & 32

Seaplanes/ Application

Rule 31: Seaplanes

What It Says

Where it is impracticable for a seaplane to exhibit lights and shapes of the characteristics or in the positions prescribed in the Rules of this Part she shall exhibit lights and shapes as closely similar in characteristics and position as is possible.

What It Means

See illustration on page 40.

PART D: Sound and Light Signals

The italicized text indicates where the Inland Rules differ substantially from the COLREGS.

Rule 32: Application

What It Says

(a) The word "whistle" means any sound signaling appliance capable of producing the prescribed blasts and which complies with the specifications in Annex III to these Regulations.
(b) The term "short blast" means a blast of about one second's duration.
(c) The term "prolonged blast" means a blast of from four to six seconds' duration.

RULE

33

Equipment for Sound Signals

What It Means

Short blast: one second (•)

Prolonged blast: four to six seconds (—)

Whistle: sound device meeting the following specifications.

LENGTH	HERTZ	DECIBELS	RANGE
12≤20 m	280–700 (250–525)	120	0.5nm
20≤75m	280–700 (250–525)	130	1.0nm

Rule 33: Equipment for Sound Signals

What It Says

(a) A vessel of 12 meters or more in length shall be provided with a whistle and a bell and a vessel of 100 meters or more in length shall, in addition, be provided with a gong, the tone and sound of which cannot be confused with that of the bell. The whistle, bell and gong shall comply with the specifications in Annex III to these Regulations. The bell or gong or both may be replaced by other equipment having the same respective sound characteristics, provided that manual sounding of the prescribed signals shall always be possible.

(b) A vessel of less than 12 meters in length shall not be obliged to carry the sound-signaling appliances prescribed in paragraph (a) of this Rule but if she does not, she shall be provided with some other means of making an efficient sound signal.

RULE

34

Maneuvering and Warning Signals

What It Means

The type of required sound-making apparatus depends on the length of the vessel.

Length	Any	Whistle	Bell	Gong
<12m	✔			
12 to <100m		✔	✔	
≥100m		✔	✔	✔

Rule 34: Maneuvering and Warning Signals

What It Says

(a) When vessels are in sight of one another, a power-driven vessel underway, when maneuvering as authorized or required by these Rules, shall indicate that maneuver by the following signals on her whistle:

—one short blast to mean "I am altering my course to starboard";

—two short blasts to mean "I am altering my course to port";

—three short blasts to mean "I am operating astern propulsion."

(b) Any vessel may supplement the whistle signals prescribed in paragraph (a) of this Rule by light signals, repeated as appropriate, while the maneuver is being carried out:

(i) these light signals shall have the following significance:

— one flash to mean "I am altering my course to starboard";

— two flashes to mean "I am altering my course to port";

— three flashes to mean "I am operating astern propulsion";

(ii) the duration of each flash shall be about one second, the interval between flashes shall be about one second, and the interval between successive signals shall be not less than ten seconds;

(iii) the light used for this signal shall, if fitted, be an all-round white light, visible at a minimum range of 5 miles, and shall comply with the provisions of Annex I to these Regulations.

(c) When in sight of one another in a narrow channel or fairway:

(i) a vessel intending to overtake another shall in compliance with Rule 9(e)(i) indicate her intention by the following signals on her whistle:

— two prolonged blasts followed by one short blast to mean "I intend to overtake you on your starboard side";
— two prolonged blasts followed by two short blasts to mean "I intend to overtake you on your port side."
(ii) the vessel about to be overtaken when acting in accordance with Rule 9(e)(i) shall indicate her agreement by the following signal on her whistle:
— one prolonged, one short, one prolonged and one short blast, in that order.

(d) When vessels in sight of one another are approaching each other and from any cause either vessel fails to understand the intentions or actions of the other, or is in doubt whether sufficient action is being taken by the other to avoid collision, the vessel in doubt shall immediately indicate such doubt by giving at least five short and rapid blasts on the whistle. Such signal may be supplemented by a light signal of at least five short and rapid flashes.

(e) A vessel nearing a bend or an area of a channel or fairway where other vessels may be obscured by an intervening obstruction shall sound one prolonged blast. Such signal shall be answered with a prolonged blast by any approaching vessel that may be within hearing around the bend or behind the intervening obstruction.

(f) If whistles are fitted on a vessel at a distance apart of more than 100 meters, one whistle only shall be used for giving maneuvering and warning signals.

(a) When power-driven vessels are in sight of one another and meeting or crossing at a distance within half a mile of each other, each vessel underway, when maneuvering as authorized or required by these Rules:

(i) shall indicate that maneuver by the following signals on her whistle: one short blast to mean "I intend to leave you on my port side"; two short blasts to mean "I intend to leave you on my starboard side"; and three short blasts to mean "I am operating astern propulsion."

(ii) upon hearing the one or two blast signal of the other shall, if in agreement, sound the same whistle signal and take the steps necessary to effect a safe passing. If, however, from any cause, the vessel doubts the safety of the proposed maneuver, she shall sound the danger signal specified in paragraph (d) of this Rule and each vessel shall take appropriate precautionary action until a safe passing agreement is made.

(b) A vessel may supplement the whistle signals prescribed in paragraph (a) of this Rule by light signals:

(i) These signals shall have the following significance: one flash to mean "I intend to leave you on my port side"; two flashes to mean "I intend to leave you on my starboard side"; three flashes to mean "I am operating astern propulsion";

(ii) The duration of each flash shall be about 1 second; and

(iii) The light used for this signal shall, if fitted, be one all-round white or yellow light, visible at a minimum range of 2 miles, synchronized with the whistle, and shall comply with the provisions of Annex I to these Rules.

(c) When in sight of one another:

(i) a power-driven vessel intending to overtake another power-driven vessel shall indicate her intention by the following signals on her whistle: one short blast to mean "I intend to overtake you on your starboard side"; two short blasts to mean "I intend to overtake you on your port side"; and

(ii) the power-driven vessel about to be overtaken shall, if in agreement, sound a similar sound signal. If in doubt she shall sound the danger signal prescribed in paragraph (d).

(d) When vessels in sight of one another are approaching each other and from any cause either vessel fails to understand the intentions or actions of the other, or is in doubt whether sufficient action is being taken by the other to avoid collision, the vessel in doubt shall immediately indicate such doubt by giving at least five short and rapid blasts on the whistle. This signal may be supplemented by a light signal of at least five short and rapid flashes.

(e) A vessel nearing a bend or an area of a channel or fairway where other vessels may be obscured by an intervening obstruction shall sound one prolonged blast. This signal shall be answered with a prolonged blast by any approaching vessel that may be within hearing around the bend or behind the intervening obstruction.

(f) If whistles are fitted on a vessel at a distance apart of more than 100 meters, one whistle only shall be used for giving maneuvering and warning signals.

(g) When a power-driven vessel is leaving a dock or berth, she shall sound one prolonged blast.

(h) A vessel that reaches agreement with another vessel in a meeting, crossing, or overtaking situation by using the radiotelephone as prescribed by the Bridge-to-Bridge Radiotelephone Act (85 Stat. 165; 33 U.S.C. 1207), is not obliged to sound the whistle signals prescribed by this Rule, but may do so. If agreement is not reached, then whistle signals shall be exchanged in a timely manner and shall prevail.

What It Means

Maneuvering and Warning Signals in Sight (• = one-second blast; — = four- to six-second blast)

INTERNATIONAL (ACTION BEING TAKEN)		INLAND (ACTION PROPOSED TO BE TAKEN)	
MEETING OR CROSSING AND ACTION IS REQUIRED (NO ANSWER REQUIRED):		MEETING OR CROSSING WITHIN 1/2 MILE OF EACH OTHER AND ACTION IS REQUIRED (AGREEMENT BYSAME SIGNAL REQUIRED):	
I am altering course to starboard	•	*I propose leaving you to port*	•
I am altering course to port	• •	*I propose leaving you to starboard*	• •
I am operating astern propulsion	• • •	*I am operating astern propulsion*	• • •
OVERTAKING IN A NARROW CHANNEL OR FAIRWAY AND ACTION IS REQUIRED (AGREEMENT REQUIRED BEFORE ACTION):		OVERTAKING IN A NARROW CHANNEL OR FAIRWAY AND ACTION IS REQUIRED (AGREEMENT BY SAME SIGNAL REQUIRED BEFORE ACTION):	
I intend to overtake on your starboard	— — •	*I propose overtaking on your starboard*	•
I intend to overtake on your port	— — • •	*I propose overtaking on your port*	• •
I agree to be overtaken	— • — •	*I agree to be overtaken*	• *or* • •
Warning—I don't understand your intentions	• • • • •	*Warning—I don't understand your intentions*	• • • • •
Approaching a bend in a channel	—	*Approaching a bend in a channel or leaving berth or dock*	—

Rule 35: Sound Signals in Restricted Visibility

What It Says

In or near an area of restricted visibility, whether by day or night, the signals prescribed in this Rule shall be used as follows:
(a) A power-driven vessel making way through the water shall sound at intervals of not more than 2 minutes one prolonged blast.
(b) A power-driven vessel underway but stopped and making no way through the water shall sound at intervals of not more than 2 minutes two prolonged blasts in succession with an interval of about 2 seconds between them.

RULE

35

Sound Signals in Restricted Visibility

(c) A vessel not under command, a vessel restricted in her ability to maneuver, a vessel constrained by her draft, a sailing vessel, a vessel engaged in fishing *(whether underway or at anchor)* and a vessel engaged in towing or pushing another vessel shall, instead of the signals prescribed in paragraphs (a) or (b) of this Rule, sound at intervals of not more than 2 minutes three blasts in succession, namely one prolonged followed by two short blasts.
(d) A vessel engaged in fishing, when at anchor, and a vessel restricted in her ability to maneuver when carrying out her work at anchor, shall instead of the signals prescribed in paragraph (g) of this Rule sound the signal prescribed in paragraph (c) of this Rule. *(Note that this paragraph does not exist in the Inland Rules.)*
(e) *(d)* A vessel towed or if more than one vessel is towed the last vessel of the tow, if manned, shall at intervals of not more than 2 minutes sound four blasts in succession, namely one prolonged followed by three short blasts. When practicable, this signal shall be made immediately after the signal made by the towing vessel.
(f) *(e)* When a pushing vessel and a vessel being pushed ahead are rigidly connected in a composite unit they shall be regarded as a power-driven vessel and shall give the signals prescribed in paragraphs (a) or (b) of this Rule.
(g) *(f)* A vessel at anchor shall at intervals of not more than one minute ring the bell rapidly for about 5 seconds. In a vessel of 100 meters or more in length the bell shall be sounded in the forepart of the vessel and immediately after the ringing of the bell the gong shall be sounded rapidly for about 5 seconds in the after part of the vessel. A vessel at anchor may in addition sound three blasts in succession, namely one short, one prolonged and one short blast, to give warning of her position and of the possibility of collision to an approaching vessel.
(h) *(g)* A vessel aground shall give the bell signal and if required the gong signal prescribed in paragraph (g) *(f)* of this Rule and shall, in addition, give three separate and distinct strokes on the bell immediately before and after the rapid ringing of the bell. A vessel aground may in addition sound an appropriate whistle signal.
(i) *(h)* A vessel of less than 12 meters in length shall not be obliged to give the above-mentioned signals but, if she does not, shall make some other efficient sound signal at intervals of not more than 2 minutes.
(j) *(i)* A pilot vessel when engaged on pilotage duty may in addition to the signals prescribed in paragraphs (a), (b) or (g), *(f)* of this Rule sound an identity signal consisting of four short blasts.

(j) The following vessels shall not be required to sound signals as prescribed in paragraph (f) of this Rule when anchored in a special anchorage area designated by the Secretary:

(i) a vessel of less than 20 meters in length; and

(ii) a barge, canal boat, scow, or other nondescript craft.

What It Means

Sound Signals in Restricted Visibility

(• = one-second blast; — = four- to six-second blast. Repeat every two minutes, maximum.)

Power vessel making way	—
Power vessel stopped	— —
Manned tow	— • • •
Pilot vessel—optional	• • • •

Not under command, restricted in ability to maneuver, constrained by draft, sailing, fishing, towing or pushing, fishing at anchor, restricted at anchor — • •

ANCHORED:

Less than 100 meters—ring bell rapidly for five seconds every minute

Greater than or equal to 100 meters—ring bell five seconds fore, then gong five seconds aft

Additional option • — •

AGROUND:

Three distinct claps of bell + rapid five-second bell + three claps, all repeated at one minute

Vessel less than twelve meters option: any sound at two minutes

RULES

36 & 37

Signals to Attract Attention/ Distress Signals

Rule 36: Signals to Attract Attention

What It Says

If necessary to attract the attention of another vessel, any vessel may make light or sound signals that cannot be mistaken for any signal authorized elsewhere in these Rules, or may direct the beam of her searchlight in the direction of the danger, in such a way as not to embarrass any vessel. Any light to attract the attention of another vessel shall be such that it cannot be mistaken for any aid to navigation. For the purpose of this rule the use of high intensity intermittent or revolving lights, such as strobe lights, shall be avoided. *(The prohibition of strobes does not apply to Inland Rules.)*

What It Means

In attracting the attention of another vessel, you may use any light or sound signal that cannot be mistaken for any of the signals given in the Rules. The only exception is a prohibition of high intensity flashing or revolving lights, such as strobes, in the International Rules. *The prohibition of strobes does not apply to Inland Rules.*

Rule 37: Distress Signals

What It Says

When a vessel is in distress and requires assistance she shall use or exhibit the signals in Annex IV to these Regulations. *The distress signals for Inland waters are the same as those for international waters with the following additional signal described: A high-intensity white light flashing at regular intervals from 50 to 70 times per minute.*

What It Means

Vessels in distress and requiring assistance shall use one or more of the distress signals listed in Annex IV of the Rules (see page 103). *The only exception is permission to use strobes in Inland waters.*

Annex IV: Distress Signals

1. Need of assistance

The following signals, used or exhibited either together or separately, indicate distress and need of assistance:

(a) a gun or other explosive signal fired at intervals of about a minute;
(b) a continuous sounding with any fog-signaling apparatus;
(c) rockets or shells, throwing red stars fired one at a time at short intervals;
(d) a signal made by radiotelegraphy or by any other signaling method consisting of the group • • • — — — • • • (SOS) in the Morse Code;
(e) a signal sent by radiotelephony consisting of the spoken word "Mayday";
(f) the International Code Signal of distress indicated by N.C.;
(g) a signal consisting of a square flag having above or below it a ball or anything resembling a ball;
(h) flames on the vessel (as from a burning tar barrel, oil barrel, etc.);
(i) a rocket parachute flare or a hand flare showing a red light;
(j) a smoke signal giving off orange-colored smoke;
(k) slowly and repeatedly raising and lowering arms outstretched to each side;
(l) the radiotelegraph alarm signal;
(m) the radiotelephone alarm signal;
(n) signals transmitted by emergency position-indicating radio beacons;
(o) approved signals transmitted by radio communication systems, including survival craft radar transponders.
(p) a high intensity white light flashing at regular intervals from 50 to 70 times per minute.

Index